LIBRARY
SOUTHERN SEMINARY

THE
GENEVA EXPERIMENT

THE
GENEVA EXPERIMENT

By

WILLIAM E. RAPPARD

Professor at the University of Geneva ; Director
of the Graduate Institute of International Studies,
Geneva, Switzerland ; Member of the Permanent
Mandates Commission of the League
of Nations

OXFORD UNIVERSITY PRESS
LONDON : HUMPHREY MILFORD
1931

OXFORD UNIVERSITY PRESS
AMEN HOUSE, E.C. 4
LONDON EDINBURGH GLASGOW
LEIPZIG NEW YORK TORONTO
MELBOURNE CAPETOWN BOMBAY
CALCUTTA MADRAS SHANGHAI
HUMPHREY MILFORD
PUBLISHER TO THE
UNIVERSITY

PRINTED IN GREAT BRITAIN

FOREWORD

THIS little book contains the substance of four lectures delivered, in May 1931, before the London School of Economics. Although drafted after the event and appreciably expanded, the text cannot fail to bear witness to its origin. This origin is mentioned here both as an explanation and an excuse for the summary and perhaps all too synthetic treatment of an inexhaustible subject. The author is happy to seize this opportunity of expressing his warm thanks to his colleagues and friends of the London School of Economics for the kind attention with which they followed his lectures. His particular thanks are due to Professors Brierly and Manning and to Mr. Humphrey Milford for making and accepting the flattering suggestion of which the presentation in book form of these lectures is the result.

W. E. R.

CONTENTS

INTRODUCTION

IN 1908, one of Great Britain's most original and far-sighted publicists, in a book which immediately became a classic, declared:

No one now expects an immediate, or prophesies with certainty an ultimate, Federation of the Globe; but the consciousness of a common purpose in mankind, or even the acknowledgement that such a common purpose is possible, would alter the face of world-politics at once.[1]

To-day, nearly a generation later, we have not yet, it is true, a federation of the globe. There is no doubt, however, that the consciousness of a common purpose has arisen in mankind, that the possibility of such a common purpose has been acknowledged, and that, as a result, the face of world politics has been altered. This change was immediately due to the World War, and it has been, if not brought about, at least demonstrated by the formation of the nations of the world into a league based on the assumption of a common purpose.

We intend, in these pages, to consider whether this change is real and not only apparent, deep and not only superficial, lasting and not only temporary. In other words, we intend to consider whether the alteration of 'the face of world-politics' implies an alteration of the whole body, of the mind, and of the soul of mankind. For our generation and for the coming generations, there is no greater or more vital question. If not only the face, but indeed the essence of world politics are not to undergo a profound change, the future of civilization is clearly menaced.

[1] Graham Wallas, *Human Nature in Politics* (3rd ed.; London, 1927), p. 294.

Whatever future historians may finally decide about the notorious war-guilt question, which so dangerously continues to poison the international atmosphere even to-day, one thing is certain. The real culprit, whose historic responsibility will always overshadow the vanity, the stupidity, and the wickedness of individual statesmen, is the pre-war system of international relations. This system, based on the conception of untrammelled national sovereignty, rival alliances, and competitive armaments, was bound, even if served by the most pacific statesmen, sooner or later to give rise to a general conflagration. Unless that system be fundamentally altered, the same causes will inevitably produce the same consequences, and the progress of the science of destruction will see to it that a world war in future will be still more radically devastating than it proved in the past.

Our purpose is to examine the Geneva experiment with a view to discovering whether it holds out any real hope for the future. We will consider it not mainly as it was intended to be by its founders, nor as it seems to be to its friends and to its critics, nor as it pretends to be in its own official documents, nor even as it is held to be in governmental circles. We wish to consider it as the political and social reality it is to-day, mindful, of course, both of its actual achievements and failures and of the underlying forces which explain both its achievements and its failures. We hope thereby to be led to some conclusions concerning its future.

It may seem strange that the citizen of a continental country should feel called upon to present the results of his observations and reflections on the League of Nations to a British audience. Is it not bringing coals to Newcastle to dump one more book about the League on the already glutted British market? Have not the most searching investigations into the real nature of the League of Nations been published in English by politicians and scholars, many of whom are connected with the London School of Economics, at whose suggestion the present lectures were delivered? The author was, in fact, encouraged to act on this suggestion by one of them who, in an admirable study in international politics published three years ago, wrote:

The League of Nations . . . is the most ambitious piece of international, or inter-State, machinery which has yet been built and, as such, it deserves close and objective study. But such study should, in part at least, be carried out upon the spot. *A priori* judgments from a distance, or from cold print alone, are apt to be misty, pedantic, and out of scale. It is difficult to visualize the League or to estimate its qualities fairly without having visited Geneva, seen the Council, the Assembly, and the Commissions in session, apprehended the environment of human contact, negotiation, gossip, and intrigue, and made personal acquaintance with members of the League Secretariat and of the staff of the International Labour Office.[1]

With this statement I find myself in full agreement. But, as all those who are or should be interested in the League of Nations cannot possibly go to Geneva to study it on the spot, it may not be quite useless for one from Geneva, who has lived on the spot ever since the League settled there, to come to them. I come from Geneva neither as an official nor as a propagandist, but as a candid and, I hope, an impartial observer, who has had and still enjoys many opportunities for immediate and close observation.

May I dwell for a moment on this essential matter of

[1] Hugh Dalton, *Towards the Peace of Nations—A Study in International Politics* (London, 1928), p. 87.

the point of view adopted in discussions concerning the League?

An opinion on the League of Nations may be defined as a relation established between its author and its object. Now most opinions so far expressed seem more revealing in the light they throw on the author rather than on the object. When we take cognizance of the views expressed on the League by the late Lord Birkenhead, for instance, or, to quote an example chosen from the opposite intellectual pole, by my brilliant friend Professor Laski, or when we listen to Mr. Churchill discussing the Indian problem, do we not thereby gain more information on the political philosophy of Lord Birkenhead, Professor Laski, and Mr. Churchill, respectively, than on the League and India as they are?

Of course this remark applies to all opinions, including even all scientific opinions. It applies with more force, however, in the realm of the social phenomena than in that of the natural world, where objectivity is less apt to be frustrated by personal bias. It applies, however, it would seem, with peculiar force to the League of Nations. Nor is this surprising. The League of Nations to-day is still, as a rule, considered more as a programme than as an historical fact. As a programme it has been discussed for centuries, whereas as a fact it is only barely emerging upon the threshold of scientific observation. Besides, so much hangs in the balance for the welfare of mankind, that, in considering the League's real structure and its positive record of achievement, one is inevitably influenced and, indeed, often blinded by one's general outlook on affairs and, especially, by one's hopes and fears for the future of world peace.

The speakers and writers on the League of Nations,

whose opinions are most often quoted, may perhaps be brought under the head of four different types.

We have, first, the politician discussing the League either at home or at Geneva. The politician is, by definition, the champion of a national policy or the spokesman of a political party. Wishing to promote his national policy or the interests of his political party, he cannot adopt the point of view of the disinterested man of science. His utterances are, therefore, justly to be discounted by all those who are seeking for enlightenment only. It is to this circumstance that the most penetrating observations on the League are very rarely made by the greatest and most influential statesmen. It is to this circumstance also that men like the late Dr. Nansen or Professor Gilbert Murray have, in the course of the speeches delivered before the Assembly in Geneva, contributed more to the real understanding of the League than most foreign ministers of the great powers. It is to this circumstance also—and the case is peculiarly instructive—that Lord Cecil's statements made as a representative of South Africa, that is, of General Smuts, that is, in fact of himself only, are of much more permanent value for a thorough comprehension of the League than those which he uttered when, representing the government of his country, he was politically more important, but intellectually less independent.

The second type of speaker or writer on the League of Nations is the League official. No one is in a better position to know the realities of the League than one whose whole activity is devoted to its service and who has access to all so-called inside information. No one, however, is less free to speak the truth, the whole truth, and nothing but the truth. Not only is the freedom of the official limited by the administrative exigencies of his position and by his duty, not to say anything which may embarrass or displease any one of his masters in the capitals of the fifty odd states members of the League. But also his vision may be and often is narrowed by his own peculiar perspective. Together with most other human beings, the League official necessarily tends to exaggerate both the relative importance and the absolute excellence of what is to him both an ideal and a job.

Of the third type of League expert, the professional propagandist, the same may be said and, as a rule, still more truly. Both less informed and less inhibited than the League official, the average propagandist, boldly confusing his hopes and his observations, paints of the League a picture that may be admirably accurate as a definition of his own aspirations, but that is too often completely deceptive as a description of reality. The stronger one feels about, and the more one works for what should be, the greater as a rule one's incapacity to state what is.

The case of the fourth type of speaker and writer on the League of Nations is, in many ways, the most complicated and the most interesting. I refer to that of the international lawyer. Most utterances on international law have a dual character, corresponding to the dual function of the international lawyer. As these utterances are intended both to be a statement of the law as it is and a source of law to which international tribunals are expressly invited to turn for their own inspiration, the international lawyer is, by definition, both a scientific student and a creator of law. Both functions of the international lawyer are legitimate, the historic-scientific and the ethical-creative. But, of course, they should be held sedulously apart, to avoid

all confusion between statements relating to what has
been and is and pronouncements as to what should be.
In the writings of most international lawyers, however,
such a confusion is facilitated by the fact that they are
apt to insert, between their inquiries as to what is and
their demonstration of what should be, some considerations on the likely development of the one into the other.

These remarks concerning the various types of
speakers and writers on the League of Nations and their
natural bias are not made in any condemnatory spirit.
Statesmen, officials, propagandists, and lawyers are all
bound by the rules of the various professional games
they are playing. It would be absurd to blame them
for the various influences under which they stand. But
it would be no less absurd not to read their writings
with due critical caution. The student's problem is to
unveil the elusive goddess of truth and to discover her
true self beneath the variously coloured robes in which
she is successively clad by her different portraitists.
Before finally accepting the statement of any com-
mentator of the League of Nations, it is therefore well
to determine his peculiar status in order to be on our
guard against his personal, national, and professional
prejudices.

In order to allow the reader to apply this rule of
critical caution to the present author, let it be known
that he is a citizen of a small country, neutral during
the War and at present the seat of the League; that he
was a conscious although passive witness of the World
War; that he was active in promoting the entry of his
country into the League; that he subsequently became,
but no longer is, a member of the Secretariat of the
League; that he still is a member of several of the
League's committees and has served his country as a

deputy-delegate at several of the last Assemblies. He is by training an economic historian, at present interested in international affairs as a student, although not a specialist of international law. He has absolutely no conscious purpose in mind when discussing the League of Nations, except that of discovering its true nature.

As a result probably of several of these personal circumstances, he is perhaps more than most of his contemporaries impressed by the need for, as well as by the rareness and the difficulty of, impartiality in the study of international affairs. Indeed, he confesses to something in the nature of a bias in favour of impartiality, as that unpopular virtue strikes him as being a necessary condition not only of the discovery of truth, but also of the maintenance of peace.

Peace, as he sees it, is a most desirable end in itself, which cannot, however, be attained so long as men have not learned to forget their national, professional, and even aesthetic preferences when considering international phenomena. No peace is possible nor, indeed, desirable that is not just. But how is a just peace ever to be established and maintained, nay how is it even ever to be recognized as such, so long as all virtues, including international fairness, are subordinated to the cult of exclusive national patriotism?

These personal observations, which are probably almost as distasteful to the reader as they are to the author, are made not to paralyse the critical vigilance of the reader, but on the contrary to stimulate by enlightening it. The love of impartiality does not make error impossible. It can but eliminate or at least extenuate one of the possible causes of error. What is certain, on the other hand, is that impartiality is, while by no means a sufficient, at least a necessary condition of the discovery of truth.

It is our intention, in the following pages, to ascertain the true character of the League of Nations. In the first chapter, we shall see what relevant information can be gleaned from the text of the Covenant and from the preceding discussions of its framers. The real answer to the question, however, must depend on the record of the League more than on its constitution. Accordingly it is hoped that the three other chapters into which this book is divided will, by outlining that record, also contribute to answer the question asked in the first. Under the heading of some outstanding constitutional developments, we shall discuss the structural changes which have taken place in the organization of the League since its foundation. We shall then proceed to a rapid analysis of the dual functions of the League, the organization of peace and the prevention of war. In a brief conclusion we propose to sum up the main results of our inquiry.

CHAPTER I

WHAT IS THE LEAGUE OF NATIONS?

THE literature dealing with the nature of the League of Nations contains an extraordinary variety of definitions. They range from the most modest, according to which the League is nothing but a novel method of international co-operation, to the most ambitious, according to which it is a complete 'denial of national sovereignty in world affairs'.

The most modest view is, perhaps, the most widely held. It is represented especially by three distinct types of individuals. We have, first, the conventional and unimaginative conservative, whose outlook on human affairs naturally tends to be somewhat cynical. For these critics, there is and can be nothing new under the sun. As human nature will ever remain what it ever has been, the League of Nations can be nothing but the transposition, upon an altered battle-field, of the age-long strife of national sovereignties.

In the second place, we have the national official of the traditional type, be he a bureaucrat or a diplomat by profession. Besides often sharing the general philosophy of observers of the first type, he is apt to be animated by an instinctive jealousy. It is the jealousy of the trained specialist towards the upstart, something akin to the feelings prevalent in many old county families towards the new rich. What are the activities of these international parvenus in Geneva, we often hear it said in these circles, if not a case of unfair and besides inefficient competition of dilettanti, deprived of both the experience and the tradition of us experts, trained in the service of our respective countries?

The political philosophy expounded by these two groups of individuals has often received support from an unexpected third quarter. We find that the progressive, but cautious international official has often expressed, if he has seldom held, similar views deprecating the importance of the League as an innovation in international affairs. Wishing the League to be successful and noting the opposition due to the spectre of a super-state which it is apt to arouse in many suspicious quarters, our international official tends to reassure public opinion by denying the essential novelty of the institution in whose service he stands. Of him one may well say what my colleague Professor Georges Scelle said of the Doyen Larnaude who, with Léon Bourgeois, constituted the French delegation to the committee which drafted the Covenant: they are 'plus prudents que sincères'.[1] Considering that the end justifies the means, they express opinions dictated more by their sense of the opportune than by their own convictions.

At the other pole of international opinion, we find the most impatient reformers. Observing that the dogma of national sovereignty has been the main stumbling-block in the path of international progress in the past, they are apt to declare, as my eminent colleague Professor Laski in the above quoted words, that the League 'is, in fact, either nothing or else a denial of national sovereignty in world affairs'.[2] Is it not possible to discover a trace of the impatience of its author in the wording of this statement itself? Is it not as if we overheard here the echo of polemic discussions?

[1] Wiktor Sukiennicki, *La Souveraineté des Etats en Droit International Moderne* (Paris, 1927), p. 297.
[2] Harold J. Laski, *A Grammar of Politics* (London, 1928), p. 228.

'If', says the ambitious reformer to the timid conservative, 'your League is not a denial of national
sovereignty, then it is nothing. As, however, we have
often condemned national sovereignty in our writings,
and as we ardently hope for the success of the League,
we deny that it is nothing, and we therefore assert that
it is a denial of national sovereignty.' Personally the
author has all the more sympathy with the members of
this progressive school, as he shares their hopes for the
future. He often finds himself unable, however, to
agree with them in their diagnosis of actual reality.
Even if one holds with them that national sovereignty
is a dangerous anachronism, which the League must
sooner or later overcome or perish, one cannot, if
realistically considering the Geneva experiment, declare
that the obstacle is already overcome. The case of Professor Laski, who enjoys a large and well-deserved
following among the younger generation, presents a
peculiar interest from the psychological point of view.
As he professes, in almost all his brilliant writings, a
pronounced dislike for the sovereign state, he seems
tempted to strike it from above by proclaiming the
existence of a super-state, as he revels in the process
of striking it from below by asserting the inalienable
rights of the individual.

Between these two extreme views, all sorts and kinds
of intermediate opinions have been expressed. The
League has been defined as a juxtaposition of states, as
a permanent conference, as an *entente*, as an alliance, as
a federation of states, and even as an embryonic federal
state. Of course, the League has also been called a commonwealth of nations, and compared with the present
status of the British Empire. It must be observed,
however, that to compare the League to the British

Commonwealth of nations, is to stress the difficulty of the problem of definition and classification more than to solve it.

If we examine all these conflicting views, we will discover that, at bottom, the controversy turns on the fundamental question of sovereignty. Let us briefly consider this problem and then show why it is crucial.

We do not attempt to recall all previous definitions of sovereignty, nor the various distinctions established between internal and external, formal and substantive, qualitative and quantitative sovereignty. Our concern is here not to complicate an already highly complicated problem, but on the contrary to simplify it by disentangling it from the mass of political, legal, and philosophical dialectics in which it has become involved.

Sovereignty is obviously not the right to do as one pleases. Even if there were no League of Nations, there could logically be room in the world for only one sovereign state, if that were the true definition of sovereignty. In fact, the limitations on national freedom resulting from the very existence of several scores of so-called sovereign states on the surface of the globe are greater than the possible additional limitations which result for any one state from its accession to the Covenant.

What we mean by national sovereignty when we ask ourselves whether the existence of the present League is compatible with that notion, is therefore not the right to do as one pleases. The question is rather whether any fundamental right of autonomous decision and action within pre-existing limits is or is not surrendered to the international community by a state when it signs the Covenant. Does a state, by joining the League, renounce its sovereignty, as did, say, the Republic of

Geneva by joining the Swiss Confederation? Does a state thereby abandon the right to conduct all its internal affairs as it pleases, and most, if not all, of its external affairs as well? Does it, in fact, remain as free from extraneous obligations as if it had not joined? Or, on the other hand, does it place itself under the control of the League?

In order to suggest an answer to these various questions, we might ask ourselves whether a state member of the League, Great Britain for instance, is governed more from its own capital, London, or more from Geneva. We might further ask ourselves what would have greater consequences for the inhabitants of Great Britain, the breakdown of the government at Westminster or of the administration in the Palais des Nations. The answer would be obvious.

Without multiplying these questions we may therefore already assert that, if sovereignty be an indivisible right, it most assuredly does not yet rest in the League, but still in its members. In the relations between the nations and the League it is obviously not the League that is preponderant, nor is there even any balance of power between the two. The preponderance still rests overwhelmingly with the state. For so-called internal matters that is undeniable. And in the present condition of international law, such questions as immigration, commercial policy, armaments, labour conditions, the status of minorities even in states bound by so-called minorities treaties, are still essentially internal matters. The only point on which a doubt is possible is in the matter of war and peace, or rather, more narrowly, in the strategy and the tactics of aggression. In this narrow but highly important field, at least for a small and isolated state, the influence of Geneva may to-day already be said to outbalance that of its national capital.

These remarks are here made in anticipation of our later conclusions. They are made here solely with a view to discovering the real nature of sovereignty as a right discussed in relation to the League of Nations. In so far as sovereignty is conceived of as political omnipotence, it is nowhere. In so far as it is conceived of as the predominant political power, it is to-day still vested in the state and only in exceptional circumstances and cases in the League.

Now, why is this matter of sovereignty the crux of the whole international position? The reply is obvious to any one who has sought to understand the obstacles encountered by the League of Nations in the realization of its major purpose. 'Either you are for Cosmopolis or you are for war,'[1] has written Mr. H. G. Wells in referring to this matter. If the League was created primarily to prevent war, as war is carried on by states, the League cannot prevent war unless it has coercive power over its member states. It may, of course, by its mere existence and by the novel possibilities of peaceful negotiation and arbitration which it offers, lessen the chances of war. It cannot, however, so long as states claim that measure of sovereignty which they still enjoy to-day, guarantee peace.

In the second place, the question of sovereignty is crucial because, if the League cannot guarantee peace, that is, protect each and all of its members against any aggression, it obviously cannot deprive them or even effectively urge them to deprive themselves of armaments. Armaments are, in the first instance, a means of national protection. So long as states continue to

[1] H. G. Wells, *The Way the World is Going* (London, 1928), p. 150.

enjoy their present sovereignty, the League, unable to guarantee peace, is necessarily also unable effectively to promote disarmament.

In the third place, if the League cannot guarantee peace, it cannot prevent the formation of alliances which, with armaments, are the traditional method of satisfying the historic need of national security.

Fourthly and finally, if the League is, as monarchy was before the end of the feudal period, without the possibility of imposing its own will, it must rely on persuasion for the promotion of its ends. It is inevitably exposed to see any collective action undertaken under its auspices blocked by the veto of any one of its members. The deeper significance of the rule of unanimity, on which the League is based, is apparent here.

The fundamental importance of the question of sovereignty may now have become apparent even to those readers who are temperamentally inclined to disregard it as too abstract or as too troublesome. The opposition between national sovereignty and international peace, to which Mr. Wells called attention in the above-quoted passage, was clearly recognized by all true thinkers and even by many politicians long before the Covenant was drafted. No one has ever recognized it more clearly, nor stated it more decisively, than Immanuel Kant, over a century ago, in his immortal essay on Eternal Peace. The following extracts will prove sufficient to show it, in spite of the characteristically involved style of the German text from which we have translated them:

Nations as states may be compared with individuals who, in the state of nature, that is as long as they are independent of external laws, threaten each other by reason of their mere juxtaposition. Therefore, if we desire to establish international security, nations must have both the right and the duty to enter into covenants comparable to those of national constitutions, in which the rights of each may be defined and secured. The result of such a step would be the creation of a league of nations which, however, would not necessarily be comparable to a state of nations. But therein lies a contradiction: as every state is based on the relation between a superior (legislative) authority and a subordinate people, a league of nations could become a state only if its members consented to become one nation. This, however, would be a contradiction in terms, as we are concerned with defining the rights of nations one to another in so far as they belong to different states and are not to be merged into one state.

When considering how savages prize their unlimited freedom, how they prefer a life of constant strife to one of submission to any legally constituted authority, and therefore prefer mad to reasonable freedom, we are filled with contempt and deem their ways uncultured, brutal, and bestially unworthy of humanity. Now one should think that civilized nations, each forming a state of its own, should hasten to escape from such an abject condition. On the contrary. We see each state placing its greatest pride and majesty in its refusal to accept any legal coercion. . . .

When a people says: 'Let there be no war amongst us, let us form a state, that is to say, let us accept a superior legislative, executive, and judiciary authority, that may peacefully settle our difficulties', that is reasonable. But when the state thus formed declares: 'There shall be no war between myself and other states, although I refuse to recognize a supreme, legislative authority which will define my right and your right', that is absolutely incomprehensible.[1]

[1] Immanuel Kant, *Zum Ewigen Frieden* (2nd ed. Leipzig, 1919), pp. 16, 17, and 20:

'Völker als Staaten können wie einzelne Menschen beurteilt werden, die sich in ihrem Naturzustande (d.i. in der Unabhängigkeit von äussern Gesetzen) schon durch ihr Nebeneinandersein lädieren, und deren jeder um seiner Sicherheit willen von dem andern fordern kann und soll, mit

In spite of Kant's ponderous language, his meaning is not only quite clear, but absolutely convincing. Either the state is free, independent, sovereign, and then assured peace is impossible; or, if one wishes to introduce law and order into international society, as it has been introduced into civil society with the advent of civilization, then the state cannot be absolutely free, independent, and sovereign.

In order to ascertain the real position of the present League of Nations on this fundamental question, let us apply the three following tests. Let us first consider the views and intentions of the framers of the Covenant. Let us, in the second place, summarily analyse the most

ihm in eine der bürgerlichen ähnliche Verfassung zu treten, wo jedem sein Recht gesichert werden kann. Dies wäre ein *Völkerbund*, der aber gleichwohl kein Völkerstaat sein müsste. Darin aber wäre ein Widerspruch: weil ein jeder Staat das Verhältnis eines *Oberen* (Gesetzgebenden) zu einem *Unteren* (Gehorchenden, nämlich dem Volk) enthält, viele Völker aber in einem Staate nur ein Volk ausmachen würden, welches (da wir hier das Recht der Völker gegeneinander zu erwägen haben, sofern sie soviel verschiedene Staaten ausmachen und nicht in einem Staat zusammenschmelzen sollen) der Voraussetzung widerspricht.

Gleichwie wir nun die Anhänglichkeit der Wilden an ihre gesetzlose Freiheit, sich lieber unaufhörlich zu balgen, als sich einem gesetzlichen, von ihnen selbst zu konstituierenden Zwange zu unterwerfen, mithin die tolle Freiheit der vernünftigen vorzuziehen, mit tiefer Verachtung ansehen und als Rohigkeit, Ungeschliffenheit und viehische Abwürdigung der Menschheit betrachten, so, sollte man denken, müssten gesittete Völker (jedes für sich zu einem Staat vereinigt) eilen, aus einem so verworfenen Zustande je eher desto lieber herauszukommen. Statt dessen aber setzt vielmehr jeder Staat seine Majestät (denn Volksmajestät ist ein ungereimter Ausdruck) gerade darin, gar keinem äusseren gesetzlichen Zwange unterworfen zu sein . . .

Dass ein Volk sagt: "Es soll unter uns kein Krieg sein; denn wir wollen uns in einen Staat formieren, d.i. uns selbst eine oberste gesetzgebende, regierende und richtende Gewalt setzen, die unsere Streitigkeiten friedlich ausgleicht,"—das lässt sich verstehen. — Wenn aber dieser Staat sagt: "Es soll kein Krieg zwischen mir und andern Staaten sein, obgleich ich keine oberste gesetzgebende Gewalt erkenne, die mir mein, und der ich ihr Recht sichere," so ist es gar nicht zu verstehen.'

important relevant provisions of the Covenant, and let us, finally, examine the activities of the League from the point of view of their bearing on the question of national sovereignty. We shall deal with the Covenant and its origins in this chapter, and reserve the analysis of the League's evolution for the latter part of this book.

The attitude of the authors of the Covenant on the question of national sovereignty may readily be determined from their written and spoken statements. As is well known, the first authoritative draft of the Covenant was that prepared by Lord Phillimore's Committee and submitted to the British Government on March 20, 1918. In the report accompanying that draft, we read the following passage which clearly shows that there was no intention on the part of its authors to encroach upon national sovereignty:

> The earlier projects which aimed at setting up a kind of European Confederation with a supernational authority we have after consideration rejected, feeling that international opinion is not ripe for so drastic a pooling of sovereignty, and that the only feasible method of securing the object is by way of co-operation or possibly a treaty of alliance on the lines of the more recent schemes.
>
> We have accordingly carefully considered those schemes, all of which substitute, in place of the earlier idea of confederation, a system working by means of a permanent conference and an arbitral tribunal.[1]

Of the various sources of the Covenant, none is more interesting than the famous Smuts Plan, published by its distinguished author under the title 'The League of Nations, A Practical Suggestion', in December 1918.

[1] David Hunter Miller, *The Drafting of the Covenant* (London, 1928), i, p. 4.

This pamphlet is characterized both by the truly prophetic vision of its remarkable author and by an extraordinary wealth and variety of ideas. As is often the case with exceptionally fertile minds, that of General Smuts does not seem always to have been dominated by a passion for consistency. So in this matter of sovereignty. On the one hand, when considering the League of Nations as the heir of the great estate of Europe which is to be liquidated, the author uses terms which seem to imply that this heir is to be endowed with all the powers of the states whose succession he is to assume. Thus we read:

The league of nations should be considered as the reversionary in the most general sense and as clothed with the right of ultimate disposal in accordance with certain fundamental principles. Reversion to the league of nations should be substituted for any policy of national annexation.[1]

In his insistence on the effective and important functions to be attributed to the League, General Smuts refers to it in such terms as 'the enduring temple of future world government' and 'the new organ of world government'. Such terms would also imply that the League, at least in so far as it was to take the place of the dismembered empires, was to inherit that measure of national sovereignty which formerly belonged to them.

On the other hand, we find in this same pamphlet statements which repudiate any such idea with still greater emphasis. Thus General Smuts writes:

Let us proceed at once to discard the idea of a super-state which is in the minds of some people. No new super-sovereign is wanted in the new world now arising. States will here be controlled not by compulsion from above

[1] David Hunter Miller, op. cit. ii, p. 27.

but by consent from below. Government by consent of the governed is our formula. The old empires were ruined by their theories of sovereignty, which meant centralization, absorption, and denationalization of the weaker national constituents of the population. The great league of nations, like the lesser league already existing in the British Empire, will have to avoid the old legal concepts of imperialism in the new world of freedom. We shall likewise have to abandon all ideas of federation or confederation as inapplicable to the case, and not likely to be agreed to by any of the existing sovereign states. We are inevitably driven to the conference system now in vogue in the constitutional practice of the British Empire, although it will necessarily have to be applied with very considerable modifications to the complex world conditions obtaining under the league.[1]

General Smuts was certainly not unconscious of the complexity of the position in which he placed himself by wishing to reconcile the decisive influence to be exercised by the League on the one hand with the refusal to grant it sovereign powers on the other. Thus, continuing his discussion of the problem, he writes:

While we avoid the super-sovereign at the one end, we must be equally careful to avoid the mere ineffective debating society at the other end. The new situation does not call for a new talking shop. We want an instrument of government which, however much talk is put into it at the one end, will grind out decisions at the other end. We want a league which will be real, practical, effective as a system of world-government. The scheme which I have seen, and which brings representatives of all the independent states of the world together in one conference to discuss the most thorny of all subjects and requires that their decisions to be binding must be unanimous, is from that point of view not worth discussion. It means that there never will be any decision issuing from the league; that nobody will take the

[1] David Hunter Miller, op. cit. ii, p. 38.

league seriously; that it will not even serve as camouflage; that it will soon be dead and buried, leaving the world worse than it found it.[1]

Without pausing further to inquire into the mysteries of the political philosophy of General Smuts, I think we may admit as a possible conciliation of his two, at least apparently, conflicting views, the following interpretation. The League, for General Smuts, was to have a double function. As the legatee of dismembered empires, it was to be endowed with powers which may fairly be termed sovereign. But as a promoter of pacific co-operation among the nations, the League was not to be very much more than a conference employing novel methods of international negotiation.

That Lord Robert Cecil, as he then was, felt the conflict between the principle of national sovereignty, on the one hand, and his desire to contribute to the constitution of an effective League, on the other, is obvious from many of his early utterances. Thus, in the speech he delivered on behalf of the British Empire delegation at the plenary session of the Peace Conference, on February 14, 1919, he declared, in commenting on the draft covenant:

As to national sovereignty we have thought, in the first place, that the League should not in any respect interfere with the internal affairs of any nation. . . .

Secondly, we have laid down, and this is the great principle in all action, whether of the Executive Council, or of the Body of Delegates, except in very special cases and for very special reasons which are set out in the Covenant, all action must be unanimously agreed to in accordance with the general rule that governs international relations.[2]

We note here a tone of reluctance which we also find

---

[1] David Hunter Miller, op. cit. ii, p. 38.   [2] Ibid. ii, p. 566.

elsewhere in Lord Cecil's statements, when alluding to the impossibility, for the present at least, to deprive states members of the League of their sovereignty.

The same attitude was doubtless that of President Wilson. As a scholar, who had devoted many years of thought to the philosophy of international relations and as an ardent promoter of the new world order in which peace was to prevail, he must have been conscious of the conflict which Kant had already so clearly defined. But as a responsible statesman, faced with the political obstacles to be overcome in establishing this order and conscious of the strength of national prejudice in the matter of sovereignty, he seems to have avoided the discussion of the problem in public. At the eleventh meeting of the Commission on the League of Nations which, on March 22, 1919, discussed an amendment to Article 8 presented by M. Léon Bourgeois, he expressly repudiated the idea of creating a super-state which that amendment seemed to involve. Referring to this meeting, Mr. David Hunter Miller writes: 'It is to be regretted that Wilson's remarks about a super-state are not fully available in his own language; but it is worth while, I think, to insert the following version from the French minutes'.[1]

In view of the importance both of the subject and of the personality of President Wilson, I may be allowed to translate this extract from the French minutes into English:

The President fears that to entrust a Commission such as that provided for in the French amendment with the duty of ascertaining whether the nations are fulfilling their duty or not would be unwelcome in many countries. It is impossible to compare such a procedure with that which might

[1] David Hunter Miller, op. cit. i, p. 320.

be permitted within the boundaries of any one state. If we were dealing with a union of states endowed with a common legislature, we might set up such a mechanism. But our idea has constantly been to discard the conception of a super-state, and that being the case it would seem difficult to provide for certain investigations within the borders of the associated nations.[1]

Although in this as in many other similar instances, the French conception of a League of Nations seemed bolder and less mindful of the rights of the sovereign state than the British, there is no doubt that at bottom official France was equally opposed to the creation of anything resembling a super-state. The following statements, extracted from the draft constitution of the League of Nations adopted by the French Ministerial Commission and considered in Paris in February 1919, are perfectly clear on this point. We read therein:

The object of the League of Nations shall not be to establish an international political State. It shall merely aim at the maintenance of peace by substituting Right for Might as the arbiter of disputes. It will thus guarantee to all States alike, whether small or great, the exercise of their sovereignty. . . .

[1] David Hunter Miller, op. cit. i, p. 320: 'Le Président craint que les visites d'une Commission analogue à celle qui est prévue dans l'amendement français pour examiner si les Nations tiennent ou non leurs engagements, ne soient mal vues dans beaucoup de pays. Pareil procédé ne peut être comparé à ce qui aurait lieu à l'intérieur d'un Etat. Si nous avions à faire à une Union d'Etats avec une législature commune nous pourrions envisager un tel mécanisme; mais, notre idée constante a été d'écarter la conception du Super-Etat et, dans ces conditions, il paraît difficile d'opérer certaines constatations à l'intérieur des Nations associées.' The English minutes of this memorable meeting are much briefer. They read as follows: 'President Wilson said that in view of the principles upon which the League was to be established, such a commission would seriously offend the susceptibilities of sovereign States. A commission to discover whether nations were keeping faith or not would certainly be unwelcome in many countries' (ii. p. 343).

There is no question of making the League of Nations a super-State, or even a Confederation. Any such idea is rendered impossible by respect for the sovereignty of States.[1]

The Italian view was not different. Signor Orlando, who presented it to the plenary session of the Peace Conference on February 14, 1919, was, like his great American colleague, both a professor of political science and a responsible statesman. The following extract from the speech he delivered on the draft Covenant on that occasion shows that he, too, had clearly recognized the difficulty:

I will rather say a few words on the general method by which we have pursued our work. The task was incomparably difficult. We started from two absolute principles which *a priori* it might seem dialectically impossible to reconcile with one another. On the one hand the principle of the sovereignty of States, which is supreme and brooks no comparison or relation, and on the other the necessity of imposing from above a restraint on the conduct of States so that the sphere of their rights should harmonize with that of the rights of all the others, in order that their liberty should not include the liberty to do evil. We were able to effect a reconciliation between these two principles on the basis of 'self-constraint', a spontaneous coercion, so that States will in future be brought, under the control of the public opinion of the whole world, voluntarily to recognize the restraint imposed on them for the sake of universal peace. I know that even the possibility of such a transformation is the object of attacks by sceptics, who are by turns sad or ironical, according to their temperament. Towards these sceptics I will act like a Greek philosopher who, when a Sophist told him that he could not move, answered by getting up and walking.[2]

[1] David Hunter Miller, op. cit. ii, pp. 238 and 243.
[2] Ibid. ii, pp. 567 and 568.

Immediately after Signor Orlando, at the same meeting, M. Léon Bourgeois spoke as follows:

Signor Orlando . . . said with unusual eloquence that there was something in the nature of a contradiction in the problem which confronted us. How were we to reconcile the principle of the sovereignty of States with the obligation by which they were to bind themselves to limit their political and military action to the precise point where Justice and Right summoned them to stop? This reconciliation has been effected, if I may say so, automatically, and, to pursue the metaphor of our distinguished colleague, we have proved the existence of motion by moving.[1]

These two speeches are extremely significant. When, after recognizing that a problem is not susceptible of a logical solution, one states that it has been solved *ambulando*, a doubt as to its effective solution is certainly permissible. But when a second advocate of the same solution of the same problem finds no other argument to adduce in its favour, we may take it that there is something distinctly wrong with the solution so unconvincingly recommended.

That the refusal of the authors of the Covenant to encroach upon national sovereignty was not a monopoly of the great powers is shown by the following extract from the minutes of the meetings held in Paris on March 20 and 21 with the representatives of the neutrals:

The Dutch Delegation raised the question of how far the constitution of the League of Nations encroached upon the sovereignty of its constituent States. They considered that it was essential that the sovereignty of individual States should not be limited.

Lord Robert Cecil said that the Commission had always considered that unless the contrary were stated in the

[1] David Hunter Miller, op. cit. ii, p. 569.

Covenant, the sovereignty of the individual States always remained intact.[1]

Another very influential member of the Drafting Committee of the Council, M. Hymans, on opening the First Assembly as temporary chairman, voiced the same opinion, expressly stating that 'the League of Nations is not, and must not be, a super-State, which aims at absorbing national sovereignties or at reducing them to wardship'.[2]

These quotations, which might be multiplied almost indefinitely,[3] clearly establish the fact that the founders of the League deliberately intended to build it up on the basis of national sovereignty. They were therefore quite consistent in recognizing that they could not absolutely exclude the possibility of war. Faced with the dilemma: maintenance of national sovereignty and possibility of war, or peace guaranteed by the subordination of the states to the League, they unmistakably and quite consciously chose the first alternative.

Thus the Phillimore Committee had already admitted that they had 'not covered all cases'[4] in their attempt to lessen the danger of war. And likewise General Smuts had declared, in his pamphlet, that 'the actual scope' of most of his proposals was 'not to prevent war altogether, but the more limited one of compelling disputants not to go to war before their dispute has been inquired into and either decided or reported upon by an impartial outside authority'.[5]

The Covenant which emerged from the labours of its

[1] David Hunter Miller, op. cit. ii, p. 623.
[2] League of Nations, Records of the First Assembly. Plenary Meetings, Geneva, 1920, p. 30.
[3] For other quotations, cf. Sukiennicki, op. cit., pp. 295 et seq.
[4] David Hunter Miller, op. cit. i, p. 5.
[5] Ibid. ii, p. 52.

drafters faithfully reflected their views on this fundamental point. We cannot, of course, attempt to analyse all its provisions here. Let us, however, hastily run through its twenty-six articles, noting first the provisions which show that the League is not a super-state, and then those other provisions in which a more ambitious tendency is sometimes discernible. The Covenant is, of course, a useful guide for the discovery of the real nature of the League, but it is so no more and no less than the constitution, say, of the British Commonwealth is a guide for the discovery of the real nature of that Commonwealth. Although 'things are seldom what they seem', in the field of political science less perhaps than elsewhere, the importance of the Covenant as indicative of the international temper of the world in 1919 should not be minimized.

That the founders of the League did not intend to set up a super-state on the ruins of the national sovereignty of its members is obvious from the following provisions:

1. In the Preamble we read that 'the High Contracting Parties, in order to promote international co-operation . . . by the acceptance of obligations not to resort to war, by the prescription of open, just and honourable relations between nations, by the firm establishment of the understandings of international law as the actual rule of conduct among Governments . . . agree', &c. Thereby they clearly indicate their will to remain their own masters in all matters not expressly mentioned in the Covenant.

2. The care with which even the appearance of the coercion of an unwilling member of the League is avoided is apparent in a great many provisions. So in Article 4, paragraph 5, providing that 'any Member of the League not represented on the Council shall be

invited . . . to sit as a Member at any meeting of the
Council during the consideration of matters specially
affecting the interests of that Member'. So also in
Article 5, paragraph 1, in which the rule of unanimity
is established. So also in the advisory and hortative
character of many vital provisions. The Council, it is
said in Articles 8, paragraphs 2 and 5; 10, 13, paragraph
4; 16 and elsewhere, is to 'formulate plans', to 'advise',
to 'recommend', to 'propose', but never to determine, to
decide, or to impose its will on reluctant members.

3. Another indication of this co-operative and non-
sovereign character of the League is to be found in the
absence of the possibility of any spontaneous initiative
from which it suffers. So, for instance, in Article 11,
paragraph 1, even in the case of an emergency such as
that created by 'war or threat of war', the Secretary-
General, on behalf of the League, can act only on the
request of one of its members. Similarly, it is provided
in paragraph 8 of Article 15 that in the case of international disputes arising 'out of a matter which by
international law is solely within the domestic juris-
diction' of one of the parties, the Council shall make no
recommendation as to their settlement.

4. If all these clear indications should not suffice, the
fact that members of the League are always at liberty to
secede from it under Articles 1, paragraph 3, and 26,
paragraph 2, would alone be decisive.

Even a cursory examination of these various provisions establishes the undeniable fact that by joining
the League a state, while accepting certain specific and
temporary obligations, does not alienate its sovereignty,
i.e. the right to remain the principal if not the sole
master of its own destiny.

On the other hand, it is quite certain that there are

also in the Covenant some significant traces of a bolder tendency than that displayed in the above-mentioned quotations. Having hitherto noted the sedulous regard for national sovereignty of the framers of the Covenant, let us now call attention to those provisions which point to the existence of a League enjoying a corporate existence not, to be sure, independent of, but at least distinct from that of its members.

1. The conditions of accession to the Covenant mentioned in Article 1 are a case in point. The mere fact that the doors of the League were left open to newcomers who could be admitted against the will of a minority of the architects of the building, points in this direction.

2. The establishment of a permanent Secretariat and of a League budget provided for under Articles 2, 6, and 7, are also symptomatic of the same tendency. In this respect the League was, from the start, endowed with a more strongly constituted corporate character than all alliances and even many confederations of the past. Thus Switzerland, for instance, before 1798, although in many respects more closely integrated than the League, disposed of neither federal personnel nor federal finances. The provisions of Article 7, paragraph 5, according to which 'the buildings and other property occupied by the League or its officials or by Representatives attending its meetings shall be inviolate', are similarly indicative of the desire to create something more than a new method of international co-operation.

3. The existence of a Council, set up under Article 4, although not provided for in the terms of reference under which the Covenant was drafted, in itself speaks for the autonomous existence of the League. It is true that, as we have seen, no real power is given to the

Council over any states not represented thereon. Still, as we shall see when examining the League in action, the Council has almost come to assume certain of the functions of a government.

4. Throughout the Covenant, we find provisions under which the Council or the Assembly or the League itself appears as saddled with responsibilities and endowed with corresponding powers independently of the individual states. So in Articles 3, paragraph 3, and 4, paragraph 4, where it is said that the Assembly and the Council 'may deal . . . with any matter within the sphere of action of the League or affecting the peace of the world'. Likewise the provision of Article 5, paragraph 2, under which all matters of procedure including the appointment of committees of investigation shall be regulated by majority vote. So especially also the provisions of the famous Article 11, which President Wilson declared to be his favourite article and which, after the rejection of the Protocol of 1924, has come to be looked upon as the backbone of the whole Covenant by most commentators.

The story of this Article 11 and particularly of the decisive provision under which, in case of war or threat of war, 'the League shall take any action that may be deemed wise and effectual to safeguard the peace of nations', is extremely interesting. In all the early drafts of the Covenant, including that published on February 14, 1919, there was no mention of any imperative duty imposed on the League as such. Instead the article merely provided that 'the High Contracting Parties reserve the right' to take the action now imposed on the League. The significant change was made in the course of a conference attended by President Wilson, Lord Robert Cecil, Colonel House, and Mr. David Hunter

Miller, on March 18, 1919. Mr. Miller informs us that Lord Robert Cecil proposed the change and that President Wilson rather unexpectedly accepted it without comment.[1] Struck with the importance of the amendment, Mr. Miller thereupon wrote to Colonel House '. . . in looking over these changes, it occurs to me that the amendment to Article 11 will tend to increase the President's difficulties with the Senate, as it makes compulsory action on the part of the League to prevent war'.[2]

Whether, as the boldest commentators now tend to suggest, the new duty thus imposed upon the League is unqualified and implies the right to take any steps necessary for the execution of that duty, or whether, as seems more plausible, the rights and duties of the League are limited by other provisions of the Covenant and notably by those defined in Article 15, the fact remains that it is difficult to reconcile the actual wording of Article 11 with the dogma of absolute national sovereignty.

5. The same is true of the provisions under Articles 10, 12, and 15, which seriously limit the freedom of members in case of war or dangerous international disputes. It is true also of the provisions of Article 16, paragraph 4, under which a member may be excluded from the League against his will. Nor is it less true of many incidental provisions of the Covenant, such as those under Article 18, providing that no treaty or international engagement shall be binding upon the parties unless registered with the Secretariat; under Article 23, that the League be entrusted with the general supervision of the execution of certain specific agreements of its members; under Article 24, that all

[1] David Hunter Miller, op. cit. i, p. 289.   [2] Ibid. i, p. 290.

international bureaux shall in future be placed 'under the direction of the League'.

6. The provisions of Article 22, dealing with mandates, deserve a special mention. Under paragraph 2 of this Article, the tutelage of the mandated areas shall be exercised 'on behalf of the League'; under paragraph 7, the mandatories 'shall render to the Council an annual report in reference to the territories committed to their charge', and under paragraph 9, a permanent Commission shall be constituted to examine these reports and 'to advise the Council on all matters relating to the observance of the mandates'. In the face of these clear provisions, it is absolutely impossible to define the League as being merely a method of international co-operation. The League in the minds of the drafters of these provisions was undeniably conceived of as enjoying a corporate existence distinct from that of its members. It is interesting to note that these provisions are the only tangible outcome of the suggestions made by General Smuts, according to which the League was to be the heir to the estate of the defeated powers.

7. Under Article 17, which deals with the relations between the League and states who have not acceded to the Covenant, the League appears in the guise of a defensive alliance of its members against the outside world. Here also it is presented as enjoying a measure of continuous, autonomous existence appreciably greater than that of a mere international conference of co-operating states.

8. Finally, the fact that under Article 26 the Covenant may be amended against the will of a minority of its signatories, shows that its character is not that of an ordinary international treaty. It is true that under paragraph 2 of this Article no amendment shall bind

any member of the League, who may always secede by signifying his dissent therefrom. Nevertheless, a League whose constitution may legally be amended against the will of a minority of its members undeniably enjoys a true corporate existence of its own.

This hasty analysis of the Covenant will suffice to show the inherent dualism which is illuminatingly characteristic of its fundamental nature. This dualism had not escaped the attention of the framers of the Covenant nor of their earliest critics. Thus we find that, during the Peace Conference, the prime minister of Australia, Mr. W. M. Hughes, in his notes on the draft Covenant, wrote on March 21, 1919:

There are two rival principles that have been set up as the foundation of a League of Nations. One is based on the idea of an international Government or Super-State; the other on the idea of a standing international Conference, or an organ of consultation.

The draft, in its main outlines, is based on the consultative idea; but it is full of expressions and phrases which suggest the governmental idea and which not only tend to obscure the proper functions of the League, but introduce a dangerous ambiguity; dangerous to the acceptance of the principle in the first place, and to its successful working if adopted.[1]

No one can quarrel with this statement. The fact is that the framers of the Covenant were constantly striving towards two distinct goals. Wishing to avoid the appearance of creating a super-state, on the one hand, they were steadfastly insisting on what may be called the co-operative idea underlying the League. But, on the other hand, wishing to avoid war or at least to reduce its dangers, they were insisting with almost equal

[1] David Hunter Miller, op. cit. i, p. 363.

force on what one might call the corporate idea of the League. Their main quest was for peace, but they consciously repudiated the logically necessary means for the achievement of that purpose, that is, the subordination of national independence to the collective will of the international community. For some of the authors of the Covenant, this repudiation was obviously inspired by the desire not to sacrifice the sovereignty of their own countries. For others and, I believe we may fairly say, for those most passionate in their desire that the League should protect humanity against war, their repudiation was based solely on grounds of expediency. It was due to their wish that the Covenant should be accepted by governmental, parliamentary, and public opinion, which was not yet ripe for the fundamental change in international relations, a change which they themselves would have accepted and perhaps indeed welcomed.

The subsequent evolution of the League to which we shall now turn illustrates a continuous conflict between the two tendencies to which we have just called attention. This conflict, as we shall see, is as yet far from being settled. As we shall submit in conclusion, it can be finally settled only by the triumph of the corporate over the co-operative idea, if peace is to prevail.

CHAPTER II

SOME OUTSTANDING CONSTITUTIONAL DEVELOPMENTS

THE drafters of the Covenant consciously refrained from doing more than to lay the foundations of the League of Nations. They wisely left it to their successors to build upon these foundations. Having in the previous chapter attempted to outline these foundations, let us now examine the superstructure. We shall thus be led to note the evolution undergone by the various organs of the League in the first twelve years of their existence.

1. *The Members of the League*

Whether we consider the League only in its co-operative aspect, or whether, with the more imaginative and forward-looking observers, we tend to stress its corporate nature, we cannot fail to agree that its most important organs are the nations which it comprises or which constitute it.

When the framers of the Covenant had concluded their labours, they expected that forty-five states would belong to the League as original members. These were the thirty-two victorious prospective signatories of the treaties of peace and the thirteen ex-neutral states invited to accede to the Covenant. The latter unanimously fulfilled the expectations of their hosts, but three of the former failed to do likewise. At the opening of the First Assembly therefore, on November 19, 1920, the membership of the League was constituted by forty-two states. To-day that number has risen to fifty-four. The following table shows both the geographical distribu-

tion and the chronological growth of this membership:

Members of the League of Nations

Continents.	Original Members.	Members admitted in:								Total.
		1920	1921	1922	1923	1924	1925	1926	1930	
Europe.	16	5	3	1	1			1		27
North America.	1									1
Central America	7	1				1				9 — 1
South America.	9									9 — 1
Asia	5									5
Oceania	2									2
Africa	2				1					3
	42	6	3	1	2	1		1		56 — 2 = 54

The two outstanding characteristics of the evolution
indicated in this table are the rapidly increased membership of the League and its striking europeanization.
Let us comment briefly upon these two characteristics.

First, this appreciably increased membership. As
President Wilson had succeeded in securing the incor-
poration of the Covenant into the peace treaties, it
seemed at least likely that the thirty-two victorious
states, on whose behalf these treaties were presented for
signature to their defeated enemies, would automatically
adhere to the League of Nations. On the other hand
there was some doubt as to the attitude of the thirteen
neutrals invited to accede to the Covenant. As to the
attitude of the defeated, there was not only doubt but
also disagreement among the victors in Paris. It may
be looked upon as one of the paradoxes of recent history
that, whereas the neutrals and the defeated European
powers have all acceded to the Covenant, three of the
victors have consistently refused to do so and that the

most important of the latter should have been the state whose spokesman was its principal author.

The only neutral powers in which the accession to the Covenant presented any difficulties were Switzerland and the Argentine Republic. In Switzerland the step was deemed to be of such fundamental importance that it was treated as a constitutional matter and therefore submitted to the procedure of the compulsory referendum. Although Switzerland had been privileged to offer the League the hospitality of its territory, and although its traditional military neutrality had been recognized by the Council as compatible with the Covenant, it was only by the most strenuous efforts and with a very slight majority that the people at the polls consented to adhere. The opposition was due mainly to the fact that the League, in 1920, resembled a somewhat enlarged *entente* rather than a true society of nations. The incomplete and therefore partial character of the League was nowhere so strongly resented as in Switzerland, where before the drafting of the Covenant there had been real enthusiasm for the fundamental principles proclaimed by President Wilson. This was due both to the strength of the tradition of neutrality in Switzerland and to the fact that two of her Germanic neighbours were among the temporarily excluded powers.

In the Argentine, whose situation has always been anomalous, the opposition to the League seems based on somewhat different grounds. Although there also the lack of universality of the League was put forward as an objection, the mention of the Monroe Doctrine, in Article 21, and the juridical inequality sanctioned by the institution of permanent members of the Council, combined with a general aversion to international entanglements, seem to have been the main factors in determining the aloofness which the great South American republic has hitherto observed.

The gradual admission of the defeated powers to the League, culminating in 1926 with that of Germany, completed an evolution which, so far as Europe is concerned at least, has made the League universal. The true universality of the League, however, is still far from being achieved. The importance of this defect as a paralysing and retarding factor in its evolution can hardly be exaggerated. The inhibitory influence of the lack of universality has made itself felt in Geneva in three distinct ways.

In the first place, certain measures of international co-operation can be adopted usefully only if they are adopted universally. It is, for instance, almost useless and therefore politically impossible, internationally to regulate such matters as the private manufacture of arms or the opium traffic, unless all states and not only the present members of the League agree on one and the same policy. It is obvious that even if one arms- or opium-manufacturing country stands out, all competing states will be reluctant to submit to any form of international restriction. The economic sacrifice inherent in any such restriction can, of course, be justified only if the aims pursued can thereby be attained. Therefore in these matters universality is an absolute condition of success.

It is true that what is referred to here is universality of co-operation and not of membership in the League. Such co-operation, irrespective of formal membership, is being increasingly pursued in Geneva. This process has, in the course of recent years, become so important that it may truly be said that the United States, for instance, is more actively and effectively engaged in promoting international co-operation in Geneva in several fields than most of the states members of the League.

The second reason why the lack of universality impedes progress is that it prevents the establishment of real international security and therefore seriously delays, even if it does not completely obstruct, the promotion of disarmament. The chain of cause and effect which unites universality and disarmament has often been noted. As Mr. J. L. Garvin declared, in 1930, in a most remarkable lecture delivered in Geneva:

By no possibility could the League of Nations have been created by Europe alone. Britain and Europe together could not have brought it about. Without America it never could have been established. Nor yet again by America without the full conviction of the British Commonwealth in the same sense and its full partnership in the work of architecture. . . .

America seceded from the League. Wilson fell. With him fell half the mass of the original peace-plan. The fall was not heaviest in the outer edifice, but within the edifice. Externally, the forms remained almost the same at Geneva. One nation amongst so many was missing. But the nation that went out was equal in weight to any twenty or thirty of the smaller nations who form half the League. Internally, half the strength of the construction had dropped out. . . .

In regard to maritime and economic sanctions, Britain, under the unamended Covenant, is still expected by some people to discharge the whole of that enormous responsibility which, when the Covenant was framed, was to be fully shared by the United States. Had America's withdrawal been foreseen that instrument would have been made subject to modification and those obligations would not have been assumed without precaution. For what now?

Changes by imperceptible degrees have brought about

what amounts, by comparison with the conditions of 1919, to an invisible revolution.[1]

Without the assurance of the loyal and effective co-operation of all the leading states of the world, in the distasteful but necessary work, or at least in the salutary threat of sanctions, there can be no loyal and effective co-operation therein on the part of the members of the League. Therefore there can be no internationally guaranteed security. Therefore even the states members of the League will continue to rely on alliances and national armaments for their own security.

In the above-quoted passage, Mr. Garvin has called attention to a third and almost equally fatal consequence of the lack of universality of the League. 'The fall', he wrote, 'was not heaviest in the outer edifice, but within the edifice.' By refusing to accept the obligations of the Covenant, a state, especially if it enjoys the economic and military power of the United States of America, not only weakens the League by withholding its own co-operation. It weakens the League perhaps still more by lessening the loyalty of the latter's members. As it remains possible for any important state to-day to secede from the League without thereby exposing itself to the dangers of isolation, the League is deprived of all real coercive influence over its members. It can always be bullied into making concessions to any one of them that threatens to withdraw unless its will be done. The story of the evolution of the Council shows that this is not merely a theoretical possibility.

The second observation which our table calls for relates to the europeanization of the League. Whereas in 1920 sixteen out of a total membership of forty-two

[1] J. L. Garvin, in *Problems of Peace* (5th series; London, 1931), pp. 259, 261, 265–6.

states were European, that proportion has increased from 38 to 50 per cent., inasmuch as to-day twenty-seven out of a total membership of fifty-four are European states. The fact that the League has become predominantly European is interesting and important in more ways than one. In itself it is not in the least surprising. Both as a promoter of international co-operation and as a safeguard against war, the League is useful to the whole world. But for Europe, the continent which is most densely populated not only by individuals but also by so-called sovereign and therefore always rival states, it has become a necessity. When one compares the statements made in the course of the successive Assemblies by representatives of European and non-European statesmen, one cannot help being struck by an obvious fact. In the evolution of international relations Europe has reached a stage where some form of effective international organization has become essential both for the prosperity and for the security of all its inhabitants. The non-European world, on the other hand, has not yet reached that stage, although it is fast tending towards it.

For the philosophically minded historian that is the true significance of the europeanization of the League which we have just noted. It also explains the plans for a European Union which, in the course of the last two years, have come to loom so large in the laboratory of the Geneva experiment. To recognize this is not, of course, to recognize the necessity or even the usefulness of that union. Were there no League of Nations, such a union would seem to be a vital necessity for the old world. Since the League has been set up, however, its dangers may well outweigh its advantages. This opinion is based on the following considerations.

In the first place, the influence of non-European states on European co-operation has, in the course of the last generation, been far more helpful than obstructive. What would be the state of Europe to-day, had there been no non-European intervention to end the World War? What would be the state of Europe to-day had there been no American co-operation in the task of reconstruction? Is it an accident that the chairmen of the two successive committees which, besides the League, have done more than any other agency to re-establish some measure of financial order in Europe, were General Dawes and Mr. Owen D. Young?

The everyday experience of the League in Geneva, whether it be engaged in the task of economic recon-struction, public health work, or political adjustments, clearly points in the same direction. Europe would be singularly ill-advised in the consideration of its own interests, as well as stupidly ungrateful, if it were to repudiate non-European co-operation in the settlement of its own affairs.

On the other hand, it is difficult to quote a single instance in which any non-European influence has blocked progress in Geneva. Except for the attitude of Brazil, which dangerously retarded Germany's entry into the League in March 1926, we know of no such instance. And the attitude of Brazil, extremely trouble-some as it was, constituted but a temporary ob-struction.

In the second place, is it not at least probable that the constitution of a European Union might tend to discourage non-European co-operation in the League of Nations? Already in the past, it has proved difficult to hold the interest of non-European states in the activities of a predominantly European League of Nations. If all

European problems should in future be submitted to the Council or to the Assembly of the League only when all the pre-consulted European states had agreed to a solution, would it not become impossible? Is it to be expected that the non-European states would long consent to play at Geneva a role so unworthy of their own importance and so offensive to their sense of national dignity?

In the third place, is there not a real danger in the constitution of a European block, based solely on grounds of geographical propinquity, that is, in the last analysis, of military power and security? It would be the first time in the world's history that the constitution of such an international block, always more or less akin to a military alliance, did not contribute to the formation of other, necessarily rival and perhaps hostile, blocks. Is a policy which opens up such vistas of danger for the peace of the world really consistent with the fundamental principles of the League?

In spite of all protests to the contrary, is it not evident, in the fourth place, that all systems of preferential rights or other economic favours such as those which are at present being envisaged in order to give Europe a new consciousness of its unity, constitute a danger for the outside world? Either such phrases as 'preferential advantages without prejudice to the interests of third states' mean nothing, and then they have the disadvantage of introducing one more element of that form of cant and insincerity into international relations which has already done so much harm in the past. Or the intentions of its authors are really to create a system of continental preferences, disregarding their own reservation, and then is it not obvious that such a policy would inevitably provoke reprisals, that is, economic war?

A fifth objection to the constitution of a European Union is that it places the British Empire before one more difficult decision, in obliging it to choose between its European and its imperial loyalty. The embarrassment which would inevitably result therefrom is not limited to Great Britain. All the smaller and even some of the larger states of the Continent view with apprehension and regret everything that tends to weaken British influence. They do so not for any sentimental but for purely national reasons, conscious of the fact that the traditional influence of Great Britain is opposed to the establishment on the Continent of any hegemony, as dangerous to themselves as it is to the British Commonwealth of nations.

A final objection to the constitution of the European Union resides in the fact that to-day almost all international problems, be they political, economic, or technical, are at bottom universal and not continental. Examples of this obvious fact are so numerous that it would be tedious to attempt to recall them. Let me quote but one as an illustration. The agricultural countries to-day, be they European, American, or Australasian, are all suffering from the over-production of grain. This at least apparent over-production is in part due to the policy of the states of Western Europe which have, with few exceptions, reduced their imports in order to promote their own production. They have done so in a large measure for considerations of national security. If the problem of the wheat surplus is to be solved, is it therefore not obvious that the solution must be political as well as economic, and universal rather than regional?

Our general conclusion is therefore that the plan of a European Union presents far more disadvantages and dangers than would appear from a casual and superficial study of the documents in which it has been presented and is being discussed. We may add that this conclusion is tacitly shared by many continentals who have been more or less silenced by the wish not to displease France or to weaken the position of her eminent foreign minister, who appear as the great champions of the idea. Doubtless every one in Europe, as elsewhere, welcomes all political and economic improvements in the mutual relations of the European countries. But the attempt to promote such improvements at the expense of international relations the world over would in our estimation be dangerous, if it were not futile.

2. *The Council*

Turning now to the history of the Council of the League, we are struck by four outstanding characteristics in its evolution since 1920.

In the first place, we note the variation in the numbers of its members. In the first stages of the drafting of the Covenant, the Executive Council, as it was then called, was modelled upon the prototype of the Supreme Council. Its membership was therefore limited to the representatives of the five victorious great powers. As the result of the protests of their smaller allies, its membership was raised first to seven and finally to nine. The idea which prevailed in the Covenant was that the great powers, while still constituting a majority, should at the same time enjoy the co-operation of four smaller states elected by the Assembly to represent the whole League. When the Council first met, its membership was reduced to eight by reason of the absence of the United States. In 1922 it was raised to ten, and in 1926 to fourteen.

It can hardly be claimed that the increased membership of the Council was due to the consciousness of any intrinsic advantages in a larger body. In 1922, as well as in 1926, the Council was enlarged primarily in order to satisfy the ambitions of impatient candidates. The change was brought about under the open or veiled threat of resignations which no friend of the League could face without serious apprehensions. Besides, the great powers which, in 1919, were first to be the sole and then the principal masters of the Council, which in 1920 were reduced to a status of numerical equality with the other states, were in 1922 placed in a minority of four to six and, in 1926, in a minority of five to nine.

Against this gradual and continuous enlargement of the Council several objections have been raised, the most obvious of which are to our mind the least real. It has been urged that the larger the Council, the more unwieldy and inefficient it would become, both on account of the difficulty of organizing its meetings to suit the convenience of all its members, and on account of the danger of deadlock in a body bound by the rule of unanimity. Nothing in the experience of the last years seems to justify these apprehensions. It has been suggested also that the enlargement of the Council might bring about the weakening of the sense of responsibility of each of its members. This objection also strikes one as being theoretical more than real.

On the other hand, there are, as we see it, two distinct disadvantages which, although not often stressed, are perhaps less imaginary. On the one hand, by enlarging the Council in order to make room for insistently impatient candidates, the League has not really lessened, but on the whole increased, the rivalry prevailing among the others, as well as the discontent of the excluded.

By postponing a perhaps inevitable crisis, it may have increased its dangers.

Already Brazil has seceded as a result of the re-organization of the Council. Is it not more than likely that the Argentine will not reassume her place in Geneva unless she is offered conditions superior to those which Brazil deemed insufficient? Turkey, likewise, has inti-mated that her national pride prevents her from joining a League in which she would not receive the recognition due to herself as a state at least as important as Poland. It is to be expected that Mexico will formulate similar demands, and it is well known that China will not indefinitely be content with her present position. That the United States of America and the Soviet Union will never join the League unless assured of a permanent seat on the Council goes without saying.

Now, if the League continued its present policy of opening the doors of the Council chamber to all states who demanded admission with sufficient insistence, the Council would immediately assume such dimensions as to make it quite unfit to exercise its normal functions. Furthermore, one fails to see a logical conclusion to such an evolution, because, if once the Council counted about twenty members, it would continue to be assailed by the demands of many if not most of the states left outside. Every one feels entitled to claim a seat in a railway coach that is considered as being a common carrier. It would therefore not seem to demand much imagination, but merely some foresight, to predict the ultimate outcome of the evolution in which the League became engaged when it took its decisions of 1922 and 1926.

On the other hand, the enlargement of the Council has already given its deliberations a character of unreality and insincerity. Every one knows that when the representatives of the great powers have agreed on a common policy on some specific point, as they frequently do in private meetings held in one or another of the Geneva hotels, the formulation of the policy of the Council on that point is not much more than a vain formality. Should any of the minor members of the Council venture to raise an objection, as they have theoretically an absolute right to do, and thus upset the apple-cart, to use a familiar phrase, their conduct would be deemed intolerable.

The divorce thus ensuing between real and formal power and between formal power and real responsibility is most unfortunate. But it is an inevitable result of the present composition of the Council. It is significant to note that the disadvantages and dangers of the present position are felt more acutely in the small states, which have apparently benefited from the increased possibilities of membership which it offers, than in great power circles. Nothing more clearly shows the contrast between appearance and reality. Now as the whole League of Nations ultimately rests on public opinion, nothing would seem to be more fatal than such antitheses between appearance and reality, because nothing more effectually undermines the confidence of the man in the street.

The second characteristic of the evolution of the Council is the diversification of its members. In the original conception of its composition, advocated by Lord Robert Cecil early in 1919, the Council was to be made up solely of permanent members. In the composition adopted by the framers of the Covenant, four non-permanent elected members were to co-operate with the five permanent members. In 1926 a third class of Council members was inserted between permanent and the non-re-eligible elected members by the establishment of the type of non-permanent, indefinitely re-eligible members.

The distinctions thus established between three types of states represented on the Council are obviously invidious. Nothing is more dangerous in international relations than the establishment of formal distinctions between states, which can be based only on the public recognition of differences in their relative importance. The danger lies in the fact that there is perhaps no single source of international conflict and even of war so poisoned as injured national pride. Considerations of prestige unfortunately dominate international relations, as considerations of personal pride and vanity still so largely dominate social relations. The supreme duty of international statesmanship is therefore to avoid any measures calculated unnecessarily to raise questions of national prestige. The diversification of the composition of the Council, which was nothing if not the formal recognition or establishment of distinctions between the relative importance of the states represented thereon, was undoubtedly a measure of this nature.

A third outstanding trait of the evolution of the Council is the increasingly active participation of its most important members in its labours. During the first years of the existence of the League, its importance and that of the Council were slight in the eyes of national foreign offices. They therefore left the preparatory work of Council sessions almost exclusively in the hands of the permanent Secretariat. As the League grew in real and universally recognized influence, an interesting change gradually came about in this respect. The instructions of Council members were discussed and prepared with far more care in the national capitals, at least in those of the European states represented on the Council. As a result, the relative influence of the Secretariat as a political agency correspondingly grew less.

Finally, and as another and more manifest result of the same cause, the Council has been appreciably modified in its personal composition, as the following table clearly shows:

Composition of the Council 1920–1931

	Number of States represented.	Number of Prime and Foreign Ministers among Council Members.	Proportion to number of Delegates.	Number of European Prime and Foreign Ministers.	Proportion to number of European Delegates.
			%		%
1920	8	11	12·7	11	16·6
1921	8	8	8	8	8
1922	8	0	0	0	0
1923	10	0	0	0	0
1924	10	9	18	9	25·7
1925	10	18	36	18	51·4
1926	10 and 14	28	43·7	28	62·2
1927	14	34	48·6	34	79·1
1928	14	30	42·8	29	72·2
1929	14	20	36·1	20	62·5
1930	14	26	46·4	25	75·8
1931	14	15	53·5	15	83·3

As is apparent from this table, it has in the course of the last years become customary for the European states members of the Council to be represented thereon by responsible members of their respective governments. The sessions of the Council have thereby come to be periodic conferences between the foreign ministers of the principal European powers.

This development, as the similar evolution we shall note below when considering the Assembly, is perhaps the most unmistakable single symptom of the growth of the League. It is obvious that the world can pay the Geneva institution no greater compliment than to delegate to its gatherings the individuals personally responsible for the conduct of foreign relations. The fact, however, is not significant only as an outward tribute paid to the growing importance of the League.

It is more significant still in its political consequences. International business can of course be more promptly and satisfactorily carried on by foreign ministers than by their delegates. Furthermore, the prolonged although intermittent presence in Geneva of those responsible for the foreign policy of most of the principal members of the international community tends to create something in the nature of an international government. Legally, each one of these national statesmen is empowered by and responsible to and for his own government only. The psychological result of their frequent co-operation as members of the Council of the League, however, is to endow them not only with a friendly *esprit de corps*, but also with a feeling of collective duty towards the League as a whole. Thus they no longer are merely representatives of their respective nations, meeting to promote and to regulate co-operative international activities. They are also coming to be representatives of the League in its own corporate existence.

3. *The Assembly*

The leading authors of the Covenant, when considering in 1919 the functions of the 'body of delegates' which, in their final draft, became the Assembly, seemed distinctly sceptical. Doubtless, they all recognized the necessity of some organ in which all the member states were to be represented. But, probably influenced by their immediate experience with the unwieldy, oratorical, and ineffective plenary sessions of the Peace Conference, they were inclined to look upon the Assembly of the League as an inevitable, but inevitably troublesome body, which it would prove expedient to summon only at rare intervals. General Smuts alone seems to have been of a contrary opinion. The pages he devotes to the future Assembly in his illuminating pamphlet are a curious and perhaps unique example of intelligent and accurate political prophecy.[1]

Already the first Assembly of the League, which met in Geneva in November 1920, foreshadowed the realization of the predictions of General Smuts. And the experience of the last decade has unmistakably confirmed the soundness of his judgement. To-day the sessions of the Assembly have come to be generally looked upon as the principal annual event in the political history of the world. When contrasted with the sceptical views of the framers of the Covenant, the effective importance assumed by the Assembly may be explained by a general consideration of the position of the League on the one hand, and on the other by three distinct decisions taken in 1920.

The general consideration we have in mind is that of the relative weakness of the League and of its Council, due to the absence of the United States. The League as a whole, and notably the body which its founders had intended to be its executive committee, proved in the first stages of their history to be appreciably less important than they had anticipated. It is therefore not

---

[1] Cf. David Hunter Miller, op. cit. ii, pp. 23 et seq. Cf. also the author's *Uniting Europe* (New Haven, 1930), pp. 205 et seq.

surprising that by contrast the Assembly proved correspondingly stronger and more important.

The three decisions to which we attribute a decisive influence in the establishment and consolidation of the Assembly's unexpected preponderance were the following. First, it was decided in 1920 that the Assembly was to meet annually. The Covenant itself, under Article 3, had provided only for meetings 'at stated intervals and from time to time as occasion may require'. In one of his drafts Lord Robert Cecil had indeed suggested quadrennial sessions.[1] The fact that the Assembly decided that its meetings should be annual indicated the intention of its members to exercise a close control over the activities of the Council and of its consultative committees. As a result of this decision, it may be said that the whole life of the League pivots on the September meetings of the Assembly. At these meetings, in view of which the Council and its subordinate bodies organize their whole activity, a yearly review of this activity, prepared by the Secretary-General, is submitted and discussed.

The second important decision was that according to which the financial existence of the League was to be based upon a budget annually discussed and approved by the Assembly. The budgetary power thus assumed by the Assembly has perhaps proved to be the greatest single factor of its preponderance. In considering this subject, one is naturally reminded of its well-known antecedents in the constitutional history of modern states. Always and everywhere it has been the power of the purse which both established and indicated the supremacy of the body that wielded it. When the power of the purse is exercised by a monarch or by a dictator,

[1] David Hunter Miller, op. cit. ii, p. 61.

we have an absolutist régime. As soon, however, as that power is assumed and effectively exercised by a parliament representing the tax-paying community, the government becomes constitutional and the reign of political liberty is established. As with national governments, so with the League of Nations.

The third element of the Assembly's importance is to be found in the publicity of its debates, the principle and the practice of which were also adopted in 1920. By thus allowing public opinion, through the press, to follow, to influence, and almost to participate in its discussions, the Assembly has in effect allied itself with the true sovereign in the contemporary world. Were the Assembly only a body of fifty national plenipotentiaries, meeting behind closed doors to scrutinize and discuss the activities of the Council, it would doubtless be overawed by the great powers, whose representatives, especially when unanimous, would dominate the League as its absolute masters. Now however that, thanks to publicity, a policy distinctly distasteful to the masses would be open to criticism in the Assembly and attack in the press of all countries by the representatives of every shade of political opinion, such a policy is never advocated in the Assembly nor, consequently, proposed even at the more secluded meetings of the Council.

The overriding and growing influence of the Assembly, which no vigilant and impartial observer of the life of the League is likely to deny, is both explained and demonstrated by the changes which have taken place in its personal composition, as shown by the table on p. 56.

What is said above with respect to the composition of the Council applies, with at least equal force, in the case of the Assembly. For the last few years, Geneva in

September may truly be said to have become something akin to the capital of the world. Not only do many of the most prominent statesmen, including often several prime ministers and usually more than a score of foreign

Composition of the Assembly 1920–1930

	Number of States represented.	Number of Prime and Foreign Ministers.	Proportion to number of Delegates.	Number of European Prime and Foreign Ministers.	Proportion to number of European Delegates.
			%		%
1920	47	6	12·8	5	23·8
1921	45	8	17·7	8	33·3
1922	48	9	18·7	9	36
1923	50	7	14	7	26·9
1924	51	22	43·1	21	80·8
1925	50	18	36	18	69·2
1926	49	18	36·7	18	69·2
1927	49	22	44·9	22	84·6
1928	50	21	42	19	70·4
1929	53	27	50·9	27	100
1930	52	29	55·8	26	96·3

ministers, assemble within its walls. But many of the world's leading publicists and journalists, financiers and captains of industry, meet there for various kinds of important interviews and conferences. As yet, as we have explained elsewhere,[1] we deem it premature to speak of world government. But here, at these periodic gatherings of many of the world's leading figures, if anywhere, we may find the embryo of the world government of the future.

When the Assembly met for the first time, one won-

[1] See the author's article entitled 'The Beginnings of International Government', in the *American Political Science Review*, vol. xxiv, No. 4, November 1930.

dered what its future would be. Was it to become merely a formal diplomatic gathering of the plenipotentiaries of the governments of the states signatories to the Covenant? Or was it to degenerate into a perhaps entertaining, but certainly ineffective, debating club? Or would it, possibly, develop into a world parliament, where the political destiny of mankind would be openly threshed out and authoritatively determined?

It is as yet too soon to answer these questions or even to discern a clear tendency in the evolution of the Assembly. That it is not, in its present state, an irresponsible debating society is obvious to any one who has attended its meetings, examined its agenda, noted its composition, or merely glanced over its debates and resolutions.

But it is difficult to say whether it is to-day more or less of a world parliament than it was in 1920. In some respects, it seems to have grown less so. The number and importance of the so-called free lances that have taken part in its debates seems to have diminished. Eminent men, unbound by governmental instructions, or spokesmen of the parliamentary opposition of the various states members of the League appear less frequently on its platform. The tone of the debates therefore seems to-day somewhat less frank and informal than it was at some of the first sessions.

This, however, may be due to the increased political importance of the League, more than to any well-defined policy to prevent the Assembly from becoming a world parliament. So long as national governments were relatively indifferent to what was said and done at Geneva, they were naturally less unwilling to be represented there by eminent individuals who, less conscious of official responsibility, were the more free to speak their own minds, irrespective of considerations of diplomatic caution and immediate political expediency. Now, on the contrary, that Geneva has become one of the strategic points on the world's chessboard, foreign offices, as the jealous guardians of national policy and national sovereignty, seem to have become less tolerant of private opinions and of individual wishes, hopes, and fears frankly expressed by their chosen representatives. The result seems to be greater caution in debate and alinements more in accordance with official national policy.

It would be premature, however, to draw any general conclusions as to the probable future of the Assembly from these observations, tentatively put forward as the impressions of a mere observer.

4. *The Secretariat*

In many respects the permanent Secretariat of the League is the most characteristic element of its structure and the most original product of its activities. Meetings of great powers, such as the concert of Europe, and international gatherings, such as peace conferences, there had been before. But in all previous gatherings of this kind, the secretarial work had been entrusted to national delegations and more particularly to the civil servants of the countries in which they met. The creation of a truly permanent international civil service, with wide and varied responsibilities, was therefore a distinct novelty.

How was this new body to be composed, constituted, and directed? Was it to be made up of national delegates, bound by national instructions and paid by national governments? Or was it to be composed of individuals, freed from all national allegiance, subjected merely to international control and paid out of a common purse?

Although much influenced in its constitution by the precedent of inter-allied bodies, which had been organized according to the first of these two conceptions, it was the second which officially prevailed in the organization of the Secretariat. It was adopted by the Secretary-General of the League, who had been chosen by the Peace Conference itself, and was officially sanctioned by the Council at one of its early meetings, in May 1920. The original policy is still in force to-day, theoretically at least, although it has not been found possible to pursue it consistently in actual practice, as recent debates have shown.

Here also, as in the deliberations of the Council and of the Assembly, the growing importance of the League has exercised a nationalizing influence. In theory the Secretary-General remains alone responsible for the choice of his associates, whose appointment to important offices has only to be confirmed by the Council. In point of fact, however, the higher and more influential positions on the Secretariat have more and more frequently come to be filled by officials drawn from the ranks of the diplomatic career, expressly recommended and sometimes even chosen by their respective governments, and therefore not unnaturally more and more conscious of their national allegiance.

This subject, which we have more fully discussed on various occasions elsewhere,[1] we shall not attempt to examine closely here. Suffice it to say that, as we see it,

[1] Cf. *Problems of Peace*, 2nd series, London, 1928, pp. 23 et seq., and 3rd series, London, 1929, pp. 16 et seq. Cf. also the minutes of the Fourth Commission of the Assembly, 1928, 1929, and particularly 1930, pp. 72 et seq.

the evolution which has taken place in the Secretariat in the course of the last decade is unmistakable, and that it was perhaps inevitable. The repeated discussions of the Fourth Committee of the Assembly and the altered spirit in the Secretariat clearly indicate that a change has taken place. That this change might have been avoided is not at all certain. In the given state of international relations and with the growing importance attached by national governments to the League, it would have been a most remarkable achievement if it had been found possible to establish and maintain a true international civil service. By such a civil service we mean one whose members would all have served the League as a whole without any special consideration to the states of which they were nationals.

Such an achievement could certainly not be expected when once the Peace Conference, after considering other possibilities, finally decided to entrust the organization and direction of the Secretariat to a national civil servant drawn from one of the great powers. This decision, due to the probably justified wish to secure for the League the backing of at least one great power, was almost bound to result in the selection, by the British Secretary-General, of immediate associates drawn from the ranks of the four other great powers which were original members of the League.

Now since the leading personalities in the Secretariat were chosen by reason not only of their individual fitness, but also on grounds of nationality, was it not futile to expect the whole civil service to be animated by sentiments of purely international allegiance? What is surprising, under the circumstances, is not that national influences should have made themselves more and more felt in the composition and in the attitude of the Secretariat, but on the contrary that it should, on the whole, have remained as free from national bias in its actual administrative work as it has in fact.

Even if the code of international ethics, expounded and insisted on by the Secretary-General on various occasions, should not have been adopted by all his associates in theory or in practice, it certainly seems to have protected them against the excesses of nationalism by which they are always threatened. Thus, in spite of certain justified criticisms, a reputation of international impartiality has been built up, which is as valuable to the League as it is creditable to those responsible for establishing and maintaining it.

5. *Technical Committees and Organizations*

After the Secretariat, the technical organizations of the League are certainly its most original structural product. These technical organizations, with their countless hosts of commissions, committees, and sub-committees, cannot be studied or even enumerated here. We are the more free not to engage in such an inquiry as it has recently been undertaken by a very well-informed British author, whose book deserves the closest study of all those who would understand what actually goes on at Geneva.[1]

Without even attempting to describe the complicated and ever-growing structure of these technical organizations, let us briefly estimate their true significance and then note the evolution which they have undergone during the last decade.

These various organizations deal with a range of topics almost commensurate with that of man's activity.

[1] H. R. G. Greaves, *The League Committees and World Order* (London, 1931).

They all, however, present certain common traits. They are all set up for the purpose of contributing to the solution on an international plane of problems which are not susceptible of a satisfactory solution when studied in one country alone, or in various countries irrespective of each other. They are all advisory in character and more or less expert in composition. In a world whose fundamental unity in the economic and social sphere is becoming ever more real and whose political diversities are being ever more stressed by the exasperation of competing nationalisms, the technical organs of the League are both a protest and a makeshift. They are a protest of the economic and social against the political. And they are a makeshift by means of which, under existing conditions, the League is attempting to give some measure of satisfaction to those demands of life and civilization which only the unification or at least the federalization of the world could adequately satisfy.

When we consider the evolution of these organizations, we are led to note the four following characteristics.

The first is their tremendous and unforeseen growth, to which the annual report of the Secretary-General to the Assembly, as well as the annual budget of the League, bear eloquent testimony. None of the authors of the Covenant, not even Lord Robert Cecil and General Smuts, who seem to have shown more interest than their colleagues in this matter, could possibly have realized the quantitative development of an element of the League's structure which was hardly foreshadowed in the Covenant. Of the scores of League committees to-day in existence, two only, the Military and the Mandates Commissions, were mentioned in that document.

A second change to be noted is their increasing specialization and diversification of function. Not only were new problems being constantly submitted to the League for study, but as the inquiries thereupon undertaken progressed, it was quite naturally found that every single topic could be almost indefinitely subdivided and usefully examined by an increasing number and variety of experts. The American definition of the specialist as a man 'who knows more and more about less and less', is fully justified by this development which will surprise no one conversant with the growing complexity and microcosmic nature of all technical problems.

A third characteristic seems to be the increasing autonomy of the technical organizations of the League. While always retaining their fundamental trait of being mainly advisory or consultative in function, they have come to be endowed by the Council and the Assembly with a growing measure of what might be called administrative self-determination. This development seems to have been due to two main causes. On the one hand, administrative convenience and efficiency demand that an expert body be not unduly hampered in its investigations by the necessity of constantly awaiting new instructions and authorizations. On the other hand, the growing co-operation of states which do not belong to the League, but which nevertheless welcome the opportunity of associating themselves in its technical work, has naturally tended to emancipate the technical organizations from the tutelage of the League's political organs.

A fourth and final change, which may be noted in at least a majority of League commissions, is the gradual substitution in their composition of the expert official or official expert for the purely private and individual specialist. This gradual change may be attributed to the increasing insistence of governments that they be at least informally represented on committees by men and women of their own choice and nationality. It is due also to the realization in Geneva of the advantages of such representation.

If the League were called upon to promote the solution of purely scientific questions, such a development would be deplorable. It is obvious that the less organizers of research are hampered by political considerations in the choice of their experts, the greater their chances of success. If, however, the problem to be solved is not merely that of discovering the truth, but of defining a policy acceptable to the governments which are to co-operate in carrying it out, then surely official experts can render greater service than private individuals, no matter how intelligent and scholarly.

The position of the official expert is, of course, always somewhat ambiguous. As an expert, his duty is not always the same as, and may indeed sometimes conflict with, his duty as an official. As an expert, he naturally tends towards the absolutely best solution of a given problem, which in most cases coincides with the interests of the human community as a whole. As an official, on the other hand, he is bound to recommend the solution most profitable, most agreeable, or perhaps merely least troublesome to his own government. As the League of Nations is a compromise between untrammelled national sovereignty and well-organized world unity, so the official expert is often the type best adapted to the special tasks which the League, in its co-operative functions, entrusts to him.

As seen from the capitals of the states members of the League, the great advantage of the expert lies in

the fact that he is both willing and qualified to defend
a national interest. When viewed from Geneva, however, his real superiority over the private expert lies
in the fact that, enjoying the confidence of his own
government, he is usually in a position to exercise some
measure of influence on the formulation of its policies.
While at Geneva he serves his government. But he may
contribute no less usefully to the final result by working
for Geneva, that is, for international co-operation, when
he returns to his national home.

6. *The Permanent Court of International Justice*

The Court at The Hague, which could not have been
set up except through the instrumentality of the League
of Nations, but which can fully carry out its special
functions only if it succeeds in completely emancipating
itself from the League, cannot be closely studied here.
Even if considerations of time and space did not forbid,
an exhaustive study of the Court could and should be
undertaken only by a trained international lawyer.

What we wish to note in this hasty inquiry into the
evolution of the structure of the League are merely two
symptoms of an apparently contradictory character.

On the one hand, it would seem to the observer who
has had an opportunity of watching the various elections
to the Court at Geneva that political influences in the
choice of judges have tended to grow stronger and not
weaker as time has gone on. An examination of the
professional records of the successful candidates would
tend to confirm the truth of this statement, based on
observations made before and during the elections
themselves.

Only a singularly naïve or an absolutely blind witness
could to-day pretend that the majority of the judges at

The Hague were chosen solely for their professional merits and in no measure by reason of their nationality and of the national preferences of their governmental electors. This development, perhaps inevitable at a period when the importance of the Court has very rapidly been enhanced by the extraordinary development of the principle of compulsory arbitration, should nevertheless be followed with critical and uneasy vigilance. If the Court is, as its founders certainly intended that it should, solely to serve the cause of international justice and to promote the progress of international law, then it should be divorced from the influence of politics as completely as is humanly feasible. Up to the present day it is impossible to deny that the development has been in the opposite direction.

On the other hand, the Court itself has clearly manifested its own desire to remain untrammelled. The regulations it has drawn up for its own guidance, its marked preference for its judicial as opposed to its advisory function, as well as the reluctance shown by the majority of its members to consider political problems or even the political aspect of the legal problems submitted to it, all go to show that the Court, when left to itself, naturally tends to assert its judicial independence. The universal desire to see the United States of America associated with the Court may have served to strengthen this tendency, as there is no country in the world whose national traditions are more favourable to the independence of the judiciary.

7. *Recapitulation*

In considering the evolution of the various organs of the League, we have everywhere been led to note the constant conflict between the principle of world unity and the dogma of national sovereignty. It is this principle that has heretofore favoured the evolution towards the universality of the League and this dogma which has constituted the principal obstacle.

It is this principle which tends to make of the Council the instrument of an embryonic world government, whereas this dogma has constantly been invoked to minimize its authority and to threaten its unity of action.

In the Assembly likewise, the struggle has been continuous, although not always manifest, between those who would tend to make of it a world parliament, representative not only of sovereign states but also of political views and economic interests, and those who insist on its fundamental character as a body of plenipotentiaries responsible solely to their respective governments.

In the Secretariat, in the technical organizations and in the Court, the conflict between the two ideals and tendencies is as real and even more obvious. We shall see, in the following two chapters, that this conflict may be noted in the functions of the League as well as in the development of its structure.

CHAPTER III

THE LEAGUE AND THE ORGANIZATION OF PEACE

ALL authors and all statesmen will agree with the man in the street that the main purpose of the League of Nations was, is, and remains the prevention of war. But all careful students of its antecedents, of its constitution, and, especially, of its history, realize that besides this, its main task, it was entrusted with a secondary duty which it has in fact persistently sought to accomplish, the organization of peace.

This duty is secondary in two ways. Not only is it secondary in importance when compared with the first, but it is secondary also in that its gradual execution tends to promote the primary purpose of the League.

This secondary task is, in itself, of a dual nature, so that one may be justified in distinguishing three functions of the League of Nations, as we have done in several of our previous writings.[1]

The organization of peace by the League of Nations comprises the execution of the peace treaties of 1919 and the promotion of international co-operation in general, quite independently of these treaties.

The terms of reference adopted by the Plenary Peace Conference in Paris, on January 24, 1919, when setting up the commission which drafted the Covenant, clearly show that these three functions were already in the minds of its authors. The relevant resolution then adopted reads as follows:

It is essential to the maintenance of the world settlement,

[1] Cf. especially *International Relations as Viewed from Geneva* (New Haven, 1925), pp. 9 et seq.

which the associated nations are now to establish, that a League of Nations be created to promote international co-operation, to ensure the fulfilment of accepted international obligations, and to provide safeguards against war.

In the definition of the purposes of the League which we find in the Preamble of the Covenant, the execution of the peace treaties is not expressly mentioned beside 'the promotion of international co-operation' and 'the achievement of international peace and security'. Nor is it, except in Article 22 relating to mandates, dealt with in the Covenant itself. It looms very large, however, both in the body of the various peace treaties themselves and in the record of the activities of the League, notably during the first years of its existence.

We have had occasion to observe that it is not considered good form among the friends of the League of Nations to mention the execution of the peace treaties among its duties. As these treaties have not, on the whole, a favourable press in the world to-day, especially in those liberal circles which tend to be most interested in the League of Nations, that is not surprising. But facts are facts, even when distasteful to some observers, and this perhaps unpalatable fact is undeniable.

It has doubtless done much to injure the cause of the League, especially in those countries in which opinion is most critical of the peace treaties. Among the nations defeated in the World War, and particularly in Germany, it has indeed been unduly stressed. The following statement made by Dr. Kastl, our former colleague on the Mandates Commission, who is assuredly one of the most reasonable of all Germans and one of those most willing to interpret the Covenant in a conciliatory spirit, may here be quoted as particularly good evidence on this point:

The Mandates Commission draws its ultimate *raison d'être* from the League of Nations, an institution which, according to a widespread conviction, was created as a means of guaranteeing the results of the World War. The League is to a certain extent endeavouring to emancipate itself from that tendency and to cure its defect of birth, but the success within the last ten years is not promising. Only if a widespread international basis for that institution can be found which excludes the application of physical force and a policy of alliances, and creates in the political world equality and an atmosphere of peace and mutual toleration, will it, perhaps, become possible to make secure the at present very uncertain existence of the Mandates Commission and to establish the ideas for which it stands.[1]

Let us, in this chapter, consider first, why this dual secondary task came to be imposed on the League of Nations and, second, how, in spite of what obstacles, in what spirit, and with what measure of success it has been carried out.

The reasons which led the founders of the League to associate it in the execution of the peace treaties are very different from those which led them to entrust it with the general duty of promoting international co-operation. They may perhaps be brought under the following four heads.

The first, and possibly the principal, reason why the Covenant was inserted into the peace treaties and the League closely entwined with many of its provisions, was to oblige reluctant parliaments to ratify the Covenant and thereby to create the League. President Wilson was no doubt more responsible for this policy than any of his colleagues in Paris in 1919.

[1] L. Kastl, in *Problems of Peace* (5th series; London, 1931), pp. 165, 166.

Although this policy was unsuccessful so far as his own country was concerned, it must to-day be generally admitted that it was essentially sound and statesman-like. Had this policy not been adopted, the League would doubtless not exist to-day. The fact that it has thereby lost some friends and gained many enemies should not lead one to forget that it would, otherwise, have probably been deprived of its very existence. Is it not obvious to-day that, in the state of discontent, disgruntlement, and, indeed, of international fury in which the Peace Conference left the nations of the world, the League could never have been set up, had the necessity of ratifying the peace treaties not obliged the parliaments of the belligerent states thereby to accede to the Covenant? It is not an enemy of the League, but one of its warmest friends and most useful servants who has recently made the following statement:

The only reason why America did not ratify the Covenant is because of the slow movement of the Senate. If every other nation had had such a slow body for ratifying treaties, very few of them would have ratified the thing. If any one had noticed what was inside, few would have ratified it. If the Covenant were put to-day as a fresh proposition to any nation in the world, it would not have a chance anywhere. That is my honest opinion.[1]

Besides, howsoever we may judge of the wisdom of the policy of securing legislative approval of the Covenant by inserting it in the peace treaties, the policy itself is undeniable.

The second motive which led the founders of the League to entrust it with the duty of carrying out the peace treaties was the wish to make of it a going con-

[1] Salvador de Madariaga, in *Problems of Peace* (5th series; London, 1931), p. 296.

cern. This is the motive which seems to have dominated
the mind of General Smuts more than that of any of
his colleagues. Conscious of the instinctive scepticism
of foreign offices and professional diplomats regarding
the possibility of maintaining peace by the establishment of a League of Nations, General Smuts had
already in his famous pamphlet, published in December
1918, insisted on the necessity of entrusting the League
with tasks which would compel the attention and assure
the co-operation of governments in its early stages. No
candid and well-informed student of the early history
of the League can deny to-day that that far-sighted
and statesmanlike policy also was fully justified by its
results.

While General Smuts was thus subordinating the
peace treaties to the League, President Wilson, more
than any of his colleagues, was anxious to use the
League in order to improve the peace treaties. In the
great speech he delivered at the plenary session of
the Peace Conference, on January 25, 1919, which
resolved to set up the League of Nations Commission,
he declared:

We have assembled for two purposes—to make the present
settlements which have been rendered necessary by the war,
and also to secure the peace of the world, not only by the
present settlement, but by the arrangements we shall make
in the Conference for its maintenance. The League of
Nations seems to me to be necessary for both of these purposes. There are complicated questions connected with the
present settlements which perhaps cannot be successfully
worked out to an ultimate issue by the decisions we shall
arrive at here. I can easily conceive that many of these
settlements will need subsequent reconsideration; that many
of the decisions we shall make will need subsequent altera-
tions in some degree, for if I may judge by my own study

of some of these questions they are not susceptible of confident judgment at present. It is, therefore, necessary that we should set up some machinery by which the work of the Conference should be rendered complete.[1]

In President Wilson's expectation, which was completely realized, it was for the League of Nations to supply this machinery.

Finally, and in addition to the three above-mentioned motives, it was discovered in the course of the laborious peace negotiations that the League of Nations provided a convenient method of overcoming the deadlocks which threatened the settlement of several delicate territorial questions. In glancing over the list of the principal tasks which have been entrusted to the League in connexion with the execution of the peace treaties, we shall find that in almost every single case they resulted from such dangerous cases of deadlock. It will be noted also that, in almost every single case, the League solutions finally adopted as a compromise were more reasonable and conciliatory than those which would otherwise probably have prevailed.

Thus in the matter of the Saar, which France wished to annex contrary to the desire of her Anglo-Saxon allies. Thus also in the case of the mandates, where the existence of the League alone prevented the outright annexation of Germany's overseas possessions and of Turkey's Arab provinces. Thus in the case of Danzig, which the League alone saved from Polish annexation. Thus also in the protection of minorities which, without the existence and intervention of the League, would doubtless have been abandoned to the arbitrary rule of their new masters.

Besides these specific cases and several others which

[1] David Hunter Miller, op. cit. ii, p. 155.

might be quoted, the very existence of the League and particularly Article 10 of the Covenant were calculated to moderate the territorial demands of the more ambitious or anxious victors. The latter were thereby offered an instrument of security in lieu of further annexations. The fact that the League, weakened by the abstention of the United States and several other circumstances, did not establish a degree of security sufficient to prevent the creation of defensive alliances and to allow for the effective reduction of national armaments, should not blind us to its real efficacy as a means of re-establishing a minimum of political confidence in Europe and thereby preventing, in the drafting of the peace treaties, errors still worse than those which were caused by the vindictiveness of the victors.

In all the above cases, in which the principles proclaimed during the war pointed in one direction, whereas historical traditions and the natural acquisitiveness of the conquerors pointed in another, the League solution was offered and accepted as a compromise. Friends of the League may deem such solutions unfortunate for the League, but they cannot fail to recognize that they were fortunate for the peace of Europe and for the nations who are condemned to inhabit that unhappy continent.

Let us turn now from the execution of the peace treaties to the promotion of international co-operation and inquire into the reasons which led the founders of the League to entrust it with this task.

That the League was not only to prevent war, but also to promote international co-operation in peace times, was an essentially British idea. Lord Robert Cecil and General Smuts, its principal advocates in 1919, as well as those of their colleagues whom they gained to their views, seem to be animated by three dominating motives.

In the first place, they deemed it expedient and indeed imperative to endow the world with a political organization adequate to its economic and social needs. It has often been said that the League was born of the World War. This statement is hardly a satisfactory explanation of the fact. Doubtless, had it not been for the World War, the League of Nations would not have been born in 1919. On the other hand, had it not been for the industrial revolution which, with all its antecedents and consequences, had for the last centuries done far more to unify the world than the war, no one would have dreamt of creating the League we know. As we have ventured to put it elsewhere,[1] it would therefore seem more accurate to say that the true mother of the League was the industrial revolution, whereas the action of the World War was rather that of a brutal midwife snatching the already conceived but still unborn babe into life.

The realization that war, from which mankind emerged in 1918, was a disease as much as a crime, which would have to be cured and not only punished, may also have contributed to the establishment of a programme of international co-operation. War, it was realized, is but a ruthless method resorted to by the strong in an endeavour to break down political barriers which seem to oppose normal evolution. If such evolution and growth can be promoted by the better organization of the world, international friction, international disputes, and war itself may perhaps be avoided. This view was stressed notably by General Smuts at the Peace Conference. It is particularly well summed up

[1] Cf. *Problems of Peace* (London, 1927), p. 46.

in the following statement, extracted from the preface of Mr. Greaves's book to which allusion has already been made:

To destroy the underlying causes of war, by constructing channels of international co-operation and by creating a disinterested viewpoint wherever national interests conflict, is vastly more important than declaring war the evil every one knows it to be. Until the organs of international disinterestedness are created, empowered, and trusted, war or the threat of war remains the necessary instrument of policy.[1]

Finally, a third circumstance was undoubtedly instrumental in saddling the League with the duty of promoting international co-operation. The state of Europe in 1919, and the urgent necessity of prolonging the salutary action of the various inter-allied bodies which had been set up during the war, made some such step imperative. These inter-allied bodies served to provide the League in its co-operative functions not only with a precedent and a technique, but also with a very valuable personnel. Thus the experience gained by such men as M. Monnet, Signor Attalico, and especially Sir Arthur Salter was most usefully placed at the service of the Geneva institution and has most fruitfully contributed to the working out of the Geneva experiment.

Having thus examined the origins of the League as an organizer of peace, let us now hastily consider the general results of its activities in this field.

In the execution of the peace treaties, the experiences of the League have been so varied and so contradictory that it is impossible to sum them up in a few sentences. We venture, however, to present the following distinc-

[1] H. R. G. Greaves, op. cit., pp. vii, viii.

tions and generalizations, based thereon, as broadly justified by the history of the past decade.

Whenever and wherever the League appeared merely as the tool of the victors, imposing their undisputed will on the defeated, the results have generally been disastrous for the League as well as for the peace of the world. The victors, it is true, may have felt some gratitude towards the League, although in general even they sometimes resented its interventions as tending to deprive them of the full fruits of their victory. The defeated, however, have been doubly incensed, not only by the losses incurred, but also by the methods employed. The neutrals, as members of the League and as impotent witnesses of its action, have been filled with grief and sometimes even with disgust. That the moral authority of the League has thereby been weakened cannot be denied.

On the other hand, whenever and wherever the League appeared, not as the tool of the victors but as the impartial representative of the world community, the results have been much more favourable.

If we review, in the light of this distinction, the history of the last decade, we shall note that, other things being equal, the earliest interventions of the League in the execution of the peace treaties were the most partial and the most vindictive. The pseudo-plebiscite of Eupen and Malmédy, which, although organized by Belgium, was sanctioned by the League early in 1920; the composition by the Council of the first Governing Commissions of the Saar, in which one fails to discover any trace of the obvious intentions of the authors of the peace treaties to secure an internationally impartial administration; and the summary method with which the complaints emanating from racial, linguistic, and religious minorities in the early days of the League were dealt with, are cases in point. The nature of the action of the Council in these and similar cases was obviously due both to the too recent memories of the World War and to the partial membership of the League, and especially of its Council, in which the influence of the neutrals was still slight, and from which the defeated were still completely absent.

We may note on the other hand that the League succeeded in appearing as a true representative of the world community in all those cases in which the factor of nationality was eliminated, or at least repressed, and in which true international impartiality was thus secured. The outstanding example is that of the supervision of the mandated territories. As the Mandates Commission was composed not of national representatives but of individuals who were responsible solely to their own conscience for the steps they recommended, their advice to the Council was, from the start, characterized by a spirit of impartiality which was recognized even in Germany. Great and lasting credit for this truly original experiment in world politics is due both to the British originators of the scheme and to the first members of the Commission who, by their courageous and impartial attitude, may be said to have set a new standard in international affairs.

The great lesson which this experiment has taught is that of the pacifying virtues of true impartiality, as opposed to the irritating influence of national partiality. As nothing excites nationalism as nationalism itself, the best method of allaying feelings of hatred between states is, whenever possible, to eliminate politics from the settlement of disputes between them. The experience of the Mandates Commission, as well as that gained by several other instances in which individuals, released from all bonds of national allegiance, have been associated in the execution of the peace treaties, has been extraordinarily enlightening. As perhaps no other single incident in the course of the last ten years, it has served to open new vistas for the future of world government.

Let us now turn to the record of the League in the promotion of international co-operation. This field has proved the most fertile of all those cultivated by the political husbandmen in Geneva. So it may well also prove the most responsive to the efforts of the disinterested student of international affairs. Speaking of this general subject in the conclusion of his interesting book devoted to the technical committees of the League, which were the main organs of this new form of international co-operation, Mr. Greaves writes as follows:

If we regard the work done by these international organs it is not difficult to appreciate its immense value and its startling novelty. Nor is it hard to estimate the point reached in the development of a world organization, to test its success by the problems that exist unsolved, and to see the tendencies in this development which appear to promise most for an eventual solution. But it may be added at once that not the most optimistic student of international relations can find the solution to be easy or sure; on the contrary even he will see that the world has moved and is still moving faster than the mechanics charged with its control. To say that it may get out of hand again at any moment is no dream of an alarmist. It is the practical view of every government that finds disarmament impossible. The truth is that the mechanic is working with equipment that is, for the most part, generations old, with instruments suited to the stagecoach in the day of the airplane, and the political plant

which supplies him would have been scrapped on principles
of efficient business generations ago. Moreover, the other
obstacles in the way of control are so great, they have so
often proved insurmountable in the most recent past, that
the future demands every effort if its uncertainty is to be
decreased.

The lesson taught by Allied experience during the war
was that continuous international agreement and co-operation on technical questions was not difficult to secure, provided that the duty of securing it were confided in specialists
more interested in their subject than in national politics and
prestige. It was discovered that direct contact between
departments of state through their ministers or officials was
more fruitful of collaboration than the formal method of
relations only through foreign offices, by diplomats trained
to regard their states as sovereign personalities of which each
single act involves the whole. And it was upon this principle
that the League's technical organization was moulded. This
discovery means much in its general implications, for it
implies that the world has found out, or is in the process
of finding out, that it does not consist of isolated units
organized for self-sufficiency and mutual competition,
having need of other isolated units only as an exception. It
means that the discovery has been made that the world
itself is the unit, with bonds that link it closely together in
every one of its functions. Such an implication has, of
course, a meaning of the most far-reaching importance to
the political organization of society. It indicates that the
theory of the sovereign state is out of line with the facts of
to-day. And it means that the organization of the world
as a political unit—unpopular though it be in certain
quarters—is the unavoidable consequence of modern conditions.[1]

With the general views expressed in this passage we
are happy to find ourselves in complete agreement. As

[1] H. R. G. Greaves, op. cit., pp. 242–4.

we have already had occasion to indicate, we agree that our pluralistic political institutions are every day proving less adequate as a framework for an increasingly monistic economic and social world. We agree also that, as a makeshift, the technical organizations of the world, based on the principle of voluntary inter-governmental co-operation, are a necessary and useful, but still an unsatisfactory, substitute for the true world institutions which are needed, but not yet wanted. We agree also, to use Mr. Greaves's felicitous metaphor, that in the airplane age we cannot hope for rapid and complete results so long as we are content to apply stage-coach methods. The League of Nations may well, and does usefully, organize relays and promote understanding concerning such matters as time-tables and standards of freight-packing. It cannot, however, replace the stage-coaches of national sovereignty by the airplanes of world unity, which the evolution of affairs ever more imperatively calls for, so long as the drivers of the stage-coaches remain in almost exclusive control.

If, analysing the various modes of international co-operation and classifying them according to their aims we seek to assess their results, we shall see that as a whole success has been in direct ratio to the immediate national advantages to be gained therefrom and in inverse ratio to the sacrifices of national sovereignty, national convenience, or national prejudice entailed. Perhaps the following classification of various types of co-operation may prove helpful.

The League has, first of all, been entrusted with the duty of organizing co-operation in several fields with the purpose of doing away with friction or of regulating competition between nations by mutual concessions. Here the obstacles have proved most formidable and progress, therefore, least encouraging. When, for instance, the League has sought to promote some measure of agreement in the matter of customs nomenclature and tariff policies, in the settlement of problems dealing with international migration, in the unification of such matters as the lighting of ships as well also, on the whole, as in the vast realm of labour conventions, it has met either with obvious failure or with a very limited measure of success.

The files of the League are full of conventions relating to these matters which have been drafted and not signed, signed but not ratified, and even when ratified not applied. They contain also many conventions which have been drafted, signed, ratified, and applied, only because their contents were insignificant.

All those who have ever been called upon to participate in the preparation of international conventions of this type are familiar with the dilemma which invariably confronts conferences summoned for that purpose. Either one inserts into the convention positive and useful provisions which, because they are calculated to assure uniformity for all, really cut into national habits. Then it is usually difficult to secure the necessary ratifications. Or, if one wishes above all to secure ratifications, one is led to render the provisions of the draft convention so elastic and so riddled with exceptions and reservations and phrases, such as 'if possible' and 'in principle', that it can satisfy only those who are content with the appearances of success.

The explanation of this dilemma is, of course, obvious. It is relatively easy, but almost completely useless, to draft international conventions which, even when faithfully applied, entail no change of national habits and customs. But if one seeks to alter such habits and customs, as one of course must in order usefully to regulate international relations and to avoid friction, one is confronted with the open protests or the passive resistance of proud and sluggish national sovereignties.

A second form of international co-operation is that in which states engage when they pursue in common a common goal. International co-operation for protection against epidemics or such collective efforts as those which led to the reconstruction of Austria and other financially weak states are cases in point. Here the sacrifices demanded of national sovereignty are less painful and the advantages to be secured more immediate. The League has therefore, as a rule, been more successful in these enterprises than in those above referred to, and its success has usually been in direct ratio to the urgency of the needs to be satisfied or the dangers to be avoided. Sir Andrew McFadyean, referring to the economic and financial work of the League, writes as follows:

It is easy to forget how near the greater part of Europe was to Bolshevism in the years immediately following the cessation of hostilities. Organized philanthropy was able to deal with the symptoms of disease, but with the drying up of that source and the disappearance of such international bodies as the Supreme Economic Council, the League provided the framework within which the causes of disease could be treated radically. The disease was a derangement of credit, with State finances in disorder and national currencies chasing each other down a primrose path to a bonfire of useless paper. The League was a rallying-point and a framework, and it provided a brain; its Financial and Economic section and its Financial Committee were a public acknowledgement that healthy finances were the *sine qua non* of healthy public and social life, and that the world was interested in, and to some degree responsible for, the prosperity of all its parts.[1]

A third form of international co-operation is that of the pursuit in common of obvious national advantages. The health work of the League is a typical example of such international co-operation. What Dr. Boudreau, one of those who has most successfully co-operated in this work, says in the following passage about the Singapore Bureau is, we believe, susceptible of a more general application:

That the Health Organization is a means of facilitating the co-operation of the different Governments in health matters is made evident by the work of the Singapore Bureau. This Bureau had behind it no international law requiring the Health Administrations to send it reports. All the cables received were the voluntary offerings of the Health Administrations, sent at their own expense. The wireless stations were also placed at the disposal of the Singapore Bureau by the different Governments. Both of these facts show that the Health Administrations are eager to collaborate in the field of international health when proper machinery is available.[2]

When we ask ourselves why the public health work of the League has been so singularly successful we shall, I believe, discover three main reasons. In the first place, it has been organized and directed, with the generous help of American finance, by Dr. Ludwig Rajchman, an international official endowed with a singularly happy and rare combination of fervent devotion, constructive imagination, and shrewd judgement.

Besides these fortunate accidents, however, the success

[1] Andrew McFadyean, in *Problems of Peace* (5th series; London, 1931), pp. 76, 77.
[2] F. G. Boudreau, in *Problems of Peace* (5th series; London, 1931), p. 115.

of the health work seems to be due also to the fact that its advantages for the states concerned are not only obvious but even statistically measurable. Even national sovereignty cannot be impervious to the lessons taught by mortality tables.

A third reason of the success of the health work seems to reside in the fact that it is of a highly technical nature and that it is therefore less exposed to the paralysing influence of politics. This last circumstance is one whose importance all those who have ever been engaged in any phase of international co-operation will readily admit. In all international conferences which have come under our observation we have always heard the same refrain. 'Keep out politics', 'leave it to the experts', 'let technical common sense prevail', such is the constant cry of those intent on prompt and effective action.

It is true that M. Briand, when presenting the idea of his European Union to the Assembly in 1928, made a memorable declaration which has sometimes been quoted in favour of the opposite thesis. What M. Briand said, when complaining of the sterility of the efforts of experts in the field of international commercial policy and when demanding the intervention of the politicians, has, it would seem, been generally misunderstood. M. Briand himself has, of course, the best of reasons for not being partial to those who command expert knowledge in any field, for not even his sincerest admirers have ever suspected him of possessing any such knowledge. What he was really criticizing, however, in the statement alluded to, was the inefficiency of expert officials whose efforts had been frustrated by drastic political instructions. The truth is that politics, that is, the pride of national sovereignty and the quest for national prestige, has ever proved the great and too often insurmountable obstacle to the progress of international co-operation.

Before closing this chapter on the organization of peace we would like to present one final observation.

When international gatherings are held, be they attended by experts or politicians or both, they are apt to be judged solely by their immediate results, i.e. the agreement reached or the convention drafted. What is often overlooked in assessing the value of such conferences is the by-product of personal acquaintance and often of confidence and even of friendship of which they have proved very fruitful. The well-informed historian of the future may well discover in this by-product an outcome of international negotiation more valuable for the improvement of international relations than the too often disappointing main product.

The fact that, thanks to the League of Nations, there are to-day in almost all states of the world influential officials, eminent lawyers, universally respected physicians, scholars, and experts of all kinds who have made friends with their opposite numbers abroad, may well in times of international crises prove to be a far more useful buttress against war than any technical treaty which they may have drawn up together.

CHAPTER IV

THE LEAGUE AND THE PREVENTION
OF WAR

THE Preamble of the Covenant reads as follows:

The High Contracting Parties,

In order to promote international co-operation and to achieve international peace and security

by the acceptance of obligations not to resort to war,

by the prescription of open, just, and honourable relations between nations,

by the firm establishment of the understanding of international law as the actual rule of conduct among Governments,

and by the maintenance of justice and a scrupulous respect for all treaty obligations in the dealings of organized peoples with one another,

Agree to this Covenant of the League of Nations.

Thus, according to this Preamble, two ends are to be pursued: the promotion of international co-operation and the achievement of international peace and security. And these two ends are to be pursued by four means: the acceptance of obligations not to resort to war, the prescription of open, just, and honourable relations, the development of international law, and the maintenance of moral standards in international affairs.

It is not quite clear whether, in the intentions of the authors, each of these four means was to contribute to the fulfilment of both the purposes of the League or not. Nor is it worth discussing. If we analyse the Covenant as a whole we will readily recognize that this armoury of peace may be said to contain the following seven distinct weapons against war:

1. the improvement of international law;
2. the improvement of international morality;
3. the reduction of armaments;
4. the consolidation of international solidarity;
5. the improvement of the procedure for the pacific settlement of disputes;
6. the limitation of the right to resort to war;
7. the principle of mutual protection.

Let us in turn examine these seven methods rapidly in order to see how they came to be forged by the framers of the Covenant and to what general use they have been put by the League.

1. *The Improvement of International Law*

International law, in its present state, is notoriously uncertain in its principles and incomplete in its scope. Furthermore, even if it were as certain and as complete as is private law in civilized communities to-day, it would suffer from a third effect inherent in all law. Law means stability, and all life implies change. Therefore, if law is to satisfy the changing needs of life, it must be susceptible of constant adaptation and progress. It is the main purpose and function of national legislatures to secure this continuous adaptation of municipal law to life.

In the international field the role of national legislatures has heretofore been played mainly by war and by the peace conferences which wars have given rise to. If international law is ever to render the international community the service which national law renders national communities to-day, it must therefore not only be made more certain in its contents and more complete in its scope, but also more readily and peacefully adaptable to the changing needs of mankind. Let us see what the authors of the Covenant have done to provide for this urgent need. The answer to this question is to be found in Articles 14, 19, 20, and 23.

Under Article 14 a Permanent Court of International Justice was set up, competent both to settle international disputes submitted to it by the parties, and to render advisory opinions at the request of the Council or the Assembly. This Court was promptly established and has been regularly functioning for the last decade.

We are not concerned with it here as a tribunal for the settlement of specific disputes, which it of course primarily is, but as an international legislator which it also is, no more and no less than law courts are legislators in national communities. While consistently refusing to expound general principles of international law, it has nevertheless, by rendering decisions in individual cases, begun to build up a fabric of jurisprudence which is bound to become a body of authoritative international law. This process in itself is doubtless destined to contribute to the better definition of international rights and obligations, and thereby to the maintenance of peace.

Under Article 19 it is provided that 'the Assembly may from time to time advise the reconsideration by Members of the League of treaties which have become inapplicable and the consideration of international conditions whose continuance might endanger the peace of the world'.

In its present wording, Article 19 represents the sadly emasculated product of the efforts of those who wished to endow the League with a real legislature. These efforts were frustrated by the still irresistible claims of national sovereignty. What was salvaged from the wreck of the original idea is not more than the expression of a need and of a hope.

It is obvious that a strictly legal interpretation of Article 19 clearly shows the futility of its provisions. In order to reach any agreement, the Assembly must be unanimous. Besides, even if unanimous, it could only advise the reconsideration of existing treaties. In order to be unanimous, it must secure the agreement of the states at whose expense treaties should be reconsidered. As, furthermore, even the unanimous advice of the Assembly could legally be disregarded by the state or states to whom it was given, Article 19 is manifestly more reassuring for the admirers and beneficiaries of the *status quo* than for the friends of progress.

When considering this article politically, and not legally, one reaches somewhat less discouraging conclusions. If, year after year, the Assembly was unanimous, or almost unanimous, in impressing upon any one of the states represented therein the advisability of the reconsideration of any treaty, the moral pressure thus exercised might in itself prove salutary. It would indeed in most cases probably prove effective, for it would be dangerous for any but the most powerful state or alliance to resist such representations. The state or group of states which was obstinate or rash enough persistently to disregard any such advice could hardly count on the support of its fellow members of the League in any emergency arising out of an attempt to secure from it by violence what it had refused to grant by peaceful negotiation.

Nevertheless the unsuccessful efforts of Bolivia, Peru, and China sufficiently show that Article 19 has not yet, in the present temper of the world, proved to be an effective means of combating war.

The third article, by means of which the authors of the Covenant intended to contribute to the improvement of international law, is Article 20. It imposes upon the states members of the League the obligation to abrogate all past engagements inconsistent with the Covenant and to refrain from entering into any such engagements in the future.

These provisions seem to have been lost sight of almost completely during the past decade. Occasionally, a polite tribute is paid to Article 20 by statesmen when referring to treaties for which they have made themselves responsible. Especially when such treaties are in the nature of special alliances difficult to reconcile with the strict interpretation of the Covenant, it is in political oratory asserted that they have been concluded in 'the spirit of the League of Nations', or 'within the framework of the Covenant'.

We fear that not a few international understandings concluded between states members of the League and duly registered by the Secretariat would hardly pass a critical examination, if investigated as to their strict compatibility with the terms of the Covenant. The fact is that here, as in many other instances, the League has shown itself to be still completely dominated by the national wills of all of its more important members. No one in Geneva has as yet ventured officially to challenge, nor is any one in particular competent to challenge, any such treaties, even when communicated to the Secretariat for registration and publication.

Finally we may mention in this connexion Article 23, which contains a whole programme of international legislation. By providing for concerted action in such

matters as labour legislation, regulation of traffic in
women and children, in opium and other dangerous
drugs, in trade in arms and ammunition, freedom of
communications and transit, equitable commercial
treatment, and prevention and control of disease, this
article has led to the negotiation of many interesting
and useful treaties. It has thus very truly contributed
to the improvement of international law.

The so far almost completely fruitless efforts of the
League in the field of what has rather unfortunately
been termed the codification of international law deserves a mention here.

These efforts have been undertaken, it would seem,
mainly with a desire to interest and to placate certain
elements of public opinion, notably in America. They
spring from a somewhat hasty desire to endow the Permanent Court of International Justice and other international tribunals with a universally accepted and well-
co-ordinated body of law which they might apply, as
national judges apply national codes. The tendency is
doubtless laudable, but in the given state of the legal
consciousness of the international community it would
seem distinctly premature.

Nor is it quite without its dangers, as the experience
of The Hague conferences, in March 1930, seems to
show. It there became very apparent that, even on
fundamental matters, states differed widely as to what
were the proper rules of international law. These differences corresponded both to the divergent national
interests of the various members of the family of nations
and to the stage of juridical civilization which they had
reached. To codify law under such conditions would
imply the levelling down of the standards of the most
advanced states to those of the least advanced, as the

concurrence of the latter would of course be indispensable and could not be otherwise obtained. The inevitable result of the desire to codify at all costs would thus be to deteriorate rather than to improve international law.

A far better and more stimulating method might be to embody in bilateral or plurilateral conventions the doctrines of the most advanced nations. While holding such conventions open to the adherence of all other states, one might then trust to time, emulation, and natural progress in order to ensure the gradual codification of international law on at least as high a plane as that already reached to-day by the most progressive nations.

2. *The Improvement of International Morality*

It was from the start one of President Wilson's fundamental convictions that no machinery could ensure peace unless nations agreed, or were taught, to behave as gentlemen. Thus in his first public utterance on the League of Nations, which we find in an address delivered before the League to Enforce Peace, in Washington, on May 27, 1916, the President of the United States already declared:

It is clear that nations must in the future be governed by the same high code of honour that we demand of individuals. . . . If this war has accomplished nothing else for the benefit of the world, it has at least disclosed a great moral necessity and set forward the thinking of the statesmen of the world by a whole age. Repeated utterances of the leading statesmen of most of the great nations now engaged in war have made it plain that their thought has come to this, that the principle of public right must henceforth take precedence over the individual interests of particular nations.[1]

This insistence on the necessity of international morality as a basis of international law and justice is characteristic of all the later American contributions to the Covenant. Thus the Preamble and Article 1 of the draft of the Covenant of the League of Nations, submitted by Colonel House on July 16, 1918, were worded as follows:

International civilization having proved a failure because there has not been constructed a fabric of law to which nations have yielded with the same obedience and deference as individuals submit to intra-national laws, and because public opinion has sanctioned unmoral acts relating to international affairs, it is the purpose of the States signatory to this Convention to form a League of Nations having for its purpose the maintenance throughout the world of peace, security, progress, and orderly government. Therefore it is agreed as follows:

Article 1. The same standards of honour and ethics shall prevail internationally and in affairs of nations as in other matters. The agreement or promise of a Power shall be inviolate.[2]

Although these provisions did not survive in the Covenant as finally adopted it does contain unmistakable traces of the views expressed therein.

Thus, in the Preamble, mention is made of 'the prescription of open, just, and honourable relations between nations', and of the 'maintenance of justice and a scrupulous respect for all treaty obligations in the dealings of organized peoples with one another'. Similarly in Article 1, paragraph 2, the admission of every new member of the League is subordinated to the

[1] President Wilson's *State Papers and Addresses* (2nd ed., New York, 1918), p. 273.   [2] David Hunter Miller, op. cit. ii, p. 7.

condition 'that it shall give effective guarantees of its sincere intention to observe its international obligations'.

The appeal to good faith in the carrying out of settlement of international disputes mentioned in Article 13, paragraph 4, as well as the solemn undertaking imposed by the League on its members not hereafter to enter into any engagements inconsistent with the Covenant, likewise testify to the ethical inspiration of the document.

The greatest practical contribution to the improvement of international morality which mankind owes the founders of the League has, however, been due to their insistence on the virtues of international publicity. This contribution was made not only by the insertion of Article 18 in the Covenant, providing for the compulsory publication of treaties, but also in the decision later taken by the Council, the Assembly, and most important League commissions and conferences, to meet in public.

At the beginning of May 1931 the number of international treaties registered with the Secretariat was 2,701. Although, as we have seen, not a few of these treaties might be held to offend against some of the fundamental principles of the Covenant, and although one may be forgiven the suspicion that all international undertakings exchanged by members of the League have not, in fact, been published in accordance with the requirements of Article 18, the principle of the compulsory publication of treaties must in itself be heralded as an important triumph of international morality. The scandal of secret treaties as legitimate instruments of policy has thus been done away with.

Greater still, however, is, in our estimation, the gain resulting from the practice of publicity which has been so largely followed in international discussions in Geneva in the course of the last decade.

But, one may ask, what connexion is there between publicity and morality? No intelligent student of international affairs will deny that that connexion is real and immediate. When treaties are kept secret, as when important diplomatic conversations are discreetly protected from the public view, the reason is often, if not always, that such treaties and such conversations, if made known to the world, would arouse the protests of the friends of justice and peace. Doubtless there may be other and more legitimate reasons for not negotiating international agreements in public. However, a convention or an understanding which is not published when once negotiated, even if its contents do not justify suspicion, inevitably arouses suspicion, and is for that reason alone destructive of international confidence, and therefore contrary to the interests of peace.

While it would be folly to look upon publicity as a substitute for morality, it is therefore most certainly a virtue in itself and one that makes for general morality. The conduct of nations as of individuals is much more apt to be blameless when open to the view and criticism of the public than when clandestine. In international politics, as in the ordinary course of human events, night favours the criminal and daylight makes for good behaviour and security, if not necessarily for saintliness.

3. *The Reduction of Armaments*

Under Article 8, paragraph 1, of the Covenant, 'the Members of the League recognize that the maintenance of peace requires the reduction of national armaments to the lowest point consistent with national safety and the enforcement by common action of international obligations'. It can hardly be said that this clause, which has perhaps been more often quoted than any other, has as yet produced any tangible effects in the status of national armaments. As we intend to revert to this all-important question in our conclusions, we will be content here to note that in the opinion of the framers of the Covenant disarmament was looked upon not only as a symptom of peace but also as a necessary condition thereof.

4. *The Consolidation of International Solidarity*

As a safeguard against war, the consolidation of international solidarity may be defined as the corner-stone of the League. Not only was it at bottom the recognition of the pacifying virtues of international solidarity that created the League itself. That recognition is made manifest also in the following specific provisions of the Covenant.

Thus Articles 3, paragraph 3, and 4, paragraph 4, providing that the Assembly and the Council may deal with any matter 'affecting the peace of the world', testify to the intentions of their authors to enlist the support of the whole international community in the effort peacefully to settle conflicts which may affect any of its members.

The same intention is manifest, and is more specifically implemented, in Article 11, which reads as follows:

1. Any war or threat of war, whether immediately affecting any of the Members of the League or not, is hereby declared a matter of concern to the whole League, and the League shall take any action that may be deemed wise and effectual to safeguard the peace of nations. In case any such emergency should arise the Secretary-General shall on the

H

request of any Member of the League forthwith summon a meeting of the Council.

2. It is also declared to be the friendly right of each Member of the League to bring to the attention of the. Assembly or of the Council any circumstance whatever affecting international relations which threatens to disturb international peace or the good understanding between nations upon which peace depends.

The main political activity of the Council, if not of the Assembly, has, since the origin of the League, been based on these provisions. In this respect, the hopes and expectations of the founders of the League have surely been fulfilled. As a conciliator and as a friendly mediator the Council has undoubtedly rendered great service to the cause of peace through the practice of international solidarity. On the other hand, it must be noted that it has never ventured to impose any solutions on members of the League parties to the dispute, to say nothing of non-members, even when the demands of justice would have called for energetic measures.

The champions of the Council, as well as its own members, are prone to attribute its extreme timidity to its wisdom rather than to its impotence. There is no doubt, of course, that in international as in all other social relations, a negotiated solution, even if reached after disquieting and troublesome delays, is usually far better than one imposed on reluctant and therefore vindictive parties. However, the conviction that the League, whatever the proper interpretation of its rights as indicated in Article 11, paragraph 1, is disinclined ever to overstep the bounds of friendly advice, and tentative recommendation is certainly detrimental to its authority as a servant of peace and still more of justice.

The provisions of Articles 13, paragraph 4, and 17, paragraph 4, under which the Council 'shall propose what steps' and 'take such measures and make such recommendations' as the situation calls for in case of persistent refusals to accept a peaceful settlement, are other examples of the intentions of the authors of the Covenant to maintain peace through the operations of international solidarity. Up to date, however, the Council has not been called upon to act in execution of either of these provisions.

5. *The Improvement of the Procedure for the Pacific Settlement of Disputes*

The procedure for the pacific settlement of international disputes is provided for under Articles 12 and 13, which deal with arbitration and judicial settlement, 14, which provides for a permanent court of international justice, and 15, which deals with mediation, conciliation, inquiry, and report by the Council. It is in these provisions that we find the rules which the founders of the League intended to serve as pacific substitutes for war. They constitute the most far-reaching innovation in international law that was attempted in Paris in 1919.

Under these provisions, no state signatory of the Covenant has the right to resort to war without first allowing for the examination and, if possible, the settlement of its dispute by a third party. This bold and statesman-like innovation may be said to have worked a revolution in the philosophy of international relations. The tremendous progress of arbitration, in the broadest sense of that elastic word, which has characterized the history of the last ten years is an outcome of this revolution.

The greatest importance of the above-mentioned articles is to be found not so much in their immediate application to international disputes as in the impetus they have given to the multiplication of bilateral and multilateral arbitration treaties, to the signing of the optional clause of the Statute of the Permanent Court of International Justice, making arbitration compulsory as between the adhering states, and to the drafting of the General Act of 1928.

A few figures may serve to give an idea of the quantitative importance of this evolution. At the beginning of May 1931 no less than 196 bilateral conciliation and arbitration treaties had been registered with the Secretariat; thirty-five states, including most of the great powers, had signed and ratified the optional clause of Article 36 of the Statute of the Court, and eight states, the number of which has increased since, had adhered to the General Act.[1] Besides, the Permanent Court of International Justice had rendered 24 judgements and 17 advisory opinions, and countless cases had been tried by arbitration tribunals, mainly by those set up under the peace treaties.

On the other hand, in spite of the great activity displayed by the Council as a mediator and as a conciliator, that body has, as above remarked, yet to assert itself as an effective agency for the pacific settlement of disputes as between parties who refuse to accept its advice.

When we look over this whole field of the League's activity we may, as so often before in the course of our inquiry, note the contrast between its success as a promoter of voluntary co-operation between the nations

[1] We are indebted for this information to M. E. Giraud, of the Legal Section of the Secretariat.

and its impotence in presence of defiant national sovereignties.

6. *Limitation of the Right to resort to War*

It is sometimes thought that the idea of combating war by eliciting from the members of the international community a solemn promise to renounce war is an invention of the authors of the Kellogg Pact. That is an entirely mistaken notion.

The Covenant itself contains several examples of such renunciation, as in the following articles:

Article 10, 'The Members of the League undertake to respect . . . as against external aggression the territorial integrity and existing political independence of all Members of the League'.

Article 12, 'The Members of the League agree . . . in no case to resort to war until three months after the award by the arbitrators or the judicial decision or the report by the Council'.

Article 13, paragraph 4, 'The Members of the League agree . . . that they will not resort to war against a Member of the League which complies' with any award or decision.

Article 15, paragraph 6, '. . . the Members of the League agree that they will not go to war with any party to the dispute which complies with the recommendations of the report'.

Furthermore, especially since the drafting of the Protocol in 1924, the successive Assemblies of the League have truly vied with one another in their repeated resolutions of renunciation.[1] If war could really be done away with by being denounced and

---

[1] Enumeration of these efforts will be found in the author's *Uniting Europe*, pp. 286 et seq.

renounced we should certainly hear no more of it to-day.

Of course, as the League has the benefit of a written constitution, its renunciations of war are necessarily couched in more specific language than that used by the authors of the Kellogg Pact. Inasmuch as the latter, however, never contemplated the prohibition of defensive warfare, their reservations and qualifications, although not so precise and specific, are not less far-reaching and thereby paralysing. If war is absolutely to be done away with, some alternative method of settling international disputes in all cases must be universally accepted. Such an alternative method, in order to be effective, necessarily implies a denial of national sovereignty. But as the nations of the world are not yet prepared to make such a sacrifice they cannot be assured of the inestimable benefit of peace, of which this sacrifice is the necessary price.

The logic of this situation was clearly brought out in the discussions of the 'Committee for the Amendment of the Covenant in order to bring it into harmony with the Pact of Paris', which sat in Geneva in the Spring of 1930. The following extract from the Minutes shows that the interrelation between the absolute prohibition of war and the compulsory settlement of international disputes was clearly recognized by the German member of the Committee:

Dr. von Bülow . . . referred to the connexion or balance between the prohibition of war and the means for the peaceful settlement of disputes. Dr. von Bülow thought the Committee would agree that there was a sort of balance between the incomplete prohibition of war and the incomplete means of peaceful settlement appearing in the Covenant.[1]

[1] Minutes of the Committee for the Amendment of the Covenant of

To this statement Lord Robert Cecil replied as follows:

He would, as a matter of historical accuracy, venture to enter a protest against Dr. von Bülow's conception of the Covenant as a highly scientific document with balances of arbitration, prohibition of war, and so on. He would very respectfully assure Dr. von Bülow that nothing could be less like the method by which the Covenant was constructed. The object had been simply to make some provision against war. As President Wilson had said, in a plenary meeting of the Conference, a foundation was being laid on which others would build. It was certainly never contemplated that a scientifically well-proportioned and well-balanced structure was being constructed.[1]

This reply, however accurate it may be historically, is logically unconvincing. Whether the framers of the Covenant were fully conscious or not of what Dr. von Bülow called 'the connexion or balance between the prohibition of war and the means for the peaceful settlement of disputes', such a connexion or balance exists in the nature of things. That is why, incidentally, it is quite impossible to close up the famous 'gaps' in the Covenant merely by introducing a few verbal amendments into that document. If you wish really and truly to renounce war, you must at the same time really and truly renounce national sovereignty in the case of a threat of war. And this neither the authors of the Kellogg Pact nor the members of the League are as yet prepared to do.

7. *Mutual Protection*

Closely allied with the consolidation of international solidarity which we have considered above is the

the League of Nations in order to bring it into harmony with the Pact of Paris, February 25 to March 5, 1930. League Document, V, Legal, 1930, V. 10, p. 17.   [1] Ibid., p. 17.

principle of mutual protection upon which the League is based and which may be mentioned as the last of the weapons against war contained in the arsenal of the Covenant.

The relevant provisions are those of Article 10, under which 'the Members of the League undertake to . . . preserve as against external aggression the territorial integrity and existing political independence of all Members of the League'; of Article 11, according to which in case of war or threat of war, 'the League shall take any action that may be deemed wise and effectual to safeguard the peace of nations'; of Article 16, which regulates the whole procedure of sanctions; and of Article 17, paragraph 3, which extends this system to the protection of members of the League against the aggression of non-member states.

None of these provisions except those of Article 11, in so far as they refer to what we have called the consolidation of international solidarity, have ever been applied. Those of Article 17, which make of the League a defensive alliance against outsiders, seems even further removed from the sphere of practical application than any of the others. To the impotence of the League in effectively organizing the mutual protection of its members we shall revert presently.

8. *Recapitulation and Conclusions*

If we now recapitulate what we have just said about the use made by the League of the seven weapons against war which we have enumerated, we might at first be tempted to draw very optimistic conclusions from our inquiry. In the course of twelve years, all but two of these weapons have in fact been employed, and often to some really useful and effective purpose. Our optimism, however, will be somewhat tempered when we consider the present position with respect to the two weapons which have been held in abeyance and which are, as a matter of fact, the most significant: disarmament and mutual protection.

The fact that the world on the whole has increased rather than reduced its armaments since the foundation of the League is susceptible of only two explanations: either these armaments have been imposed on unwilling peoples by the tyranny of dictators and the subtle intriguing of militarists and ammunition manufacturers, or they are sanctioned by the popular will.

The first of these explanations may suffice to explain certain increases of armaments. It is, however, obviously insufficient as a guide to the understanding of the present state of Europe as an armed camp. The fact is, and should be faced frankly, that the people in many if not in most democratic countries of Europe accept and, indeed, demand armaments. This proves that, still suspecting each other, they do not yet rely on the League for their protection. No renunciations of war, however eloquent and often reiterated, should blind us as to this ugly fact. As Señor de Madariaga wittily but truly remarked in the course of a lecture delivered at Geneva in the summer of 1930:

So here we go year after year depositing solemn oaths on the altar of international peace; and year after year with the other hand depositing millions on the altar of war. What does that mean? Does it mean that we are following the precept in the Gospel, which I thought applied only to pianists: 'Let not thy right hand know what thy left hand doeth'? Does it also apply to Governments? Are they signing treaties of no-war with the right hand and signing contracts of armaments with the left as hard as they can do it? [1]

As is well known, the refusal to disarm, which has been the persistent policy of most of the states of Europe, and notably of those who have most profited by the peace treaties of 1919, is ever more bitterly resented by their defeated foes. The following statement, made by one of the most reasonable of German publicists and one of the most faithful advocates of the late Mr. Stresemann's conciliatory policy, indicates the degree of exasperation which prevails in Germany to-day. In a speech delivered in Paris on March 22, 1931, the Freiherr von Rheinbaben spoke as follows:

I must have the courage to say it here. A great number of my compatriots have so far lost all confidence in the League of Nations that in public meetings, and not only in those frequented solely or partly by conservative citizens, the mere mention of the League of Nations provokes prolonged strains of ironical laughter. Let me admit that you do not doubt of what I say and you will realize that it will no longer be possible for a German Government, however loyally inclined towards international conciliation, to continue in complete and effective co-operation with the League of Nations, if the League does not fulfil the most important of its duties and cannot keep the solemn promise made in the Covenant and in the Treaty of Peace, tending towards the realization of a general parity of armaments.[2]

[1] Salvador de Madariaga, op. cit., p. 293.
[2] von Rheinbaben, 'L'Opinion Allemande et le Désarmement', in *Le Monde Nouveau*, April 1931, p. 69:
'Il faut que j'aie le courage de le dire: un grand nombre de mes compatriotes ont perdu à ce point la foi en la S.D.N. que, dans toutes les réunions publiques et non pas celles composées uniquement ou partiellement d'éléments de droite, la seule mention de S.D.N. suffit pour provoquer de longs rires ironiques. Qu'il me soit permis de supposer que vous ne mettez pas en doute ce que j'avance, et qu'il ne sera pas plus longtemps possible à la plus loyale volonté d'entente d'un

The main cause of the reluctance of certain states members of the League to reduce their national armaments is that they do not trust the League for their protection. Nor is this surprising. Cannot the story of the last decade be summed up as follows: When asked to disarm under Article 8, the nations demanded additional security. When they obtained some measure of security, as they did at Locarno, they asked for more. On the other hand, when asked to provide security under Article 16, they refused to give the required guarantees. There is, in fact, as Mr. J. L. Garvin has truly said in his above-quoted address, a 'danger of a deadlock of ideas . . . between the appeals for general disarmament and the demand for particular securities'. This tragic deadlock is due to two main reasons.

The members of the League are inhibited from granting each other the necessary measure of mutual protection because the lack of universality of the League leads them to fear external complications if they should faithfully carry out the pledges of the Covenant.

This has become increasingly clear ever since the first debate in the Council on the subject, on August 2, 1920. It was on that occasion that the Council first considered the full implications of Article 16 of the Covenant. It did so on the basis of a memorandum presented by the Secretary-General and of a report which was read by the Italian representative, Signor Tittoni.

In the memorandum of the Secretary-General we read the following statement, which shows how, in

gouvernement allemand quel qu'il soit, de maintenir, entière et efficace, sa collaboration à la S.D.N., si celle-ci ne remplit pas le plus élevé de ses devoirs et ne tient pas la promesse solennelle prévue dans le Pacte et dans le Traité de Paix, à savoir de prendre les dispositions nécessaires pour réaliser la parité générale des armements.'

those early days, the power of the League was over-estimated in the circles of its own officials:

Many people think that the League is founded more upon good intentions than upon a cool consideration of the stern realities of international trouble. It is, therefore, desirable on general grounds that while the first meetings of the Council and of the Assembly should give the world the positive hope of removing misunderstandings and promoting international co-operation, they should also show quite clearly that the Members of the League as a whole are determined, if necessity arises, to enforce their will by effective action on any particular country which, in the circumstances contemplated by the Covenant, defies the general verdict of the world.[1]

When Signor Tittoni came to present his report, in which he originally championed the same general conception, the Minutes of the meeting inform us that 'an important discussion arose on the interpretation to be placed upon the clause of Article 16 of the Covenant under which measures are to be taken by the League to prevent states which are not Members of the League from having commercial relations with a Member of the League which has broken the Covenant'.[2] The Belgian representative, M. Hymans, declared that 'a breach of the Covenant was an international crime, and all the States of the world might legitimately be asked to support the measures taken by the League to procure redress'.

M. Bourgeois, the French representative, added 'that the view taken by M. Hymans was undoubtedly the view of those who framed the Covenant'.

Thereupon Mr. Balfour, on behalf of the British

[1] Procès-Verbal of the Eighth Session of the Council of the League of Nations, held in San Sebastian, July 30 to August 5, 1920, p. 129.
[2] Ibid., p. 27.

Empire, 'pointed out that, when the Covenant was drafted, it was believed that the United States, Russia, and eventually Germany would be Members of the League. He inquired how the League was in practice to compel these States to break off relations.' This clear recognition of an obviously insurmountable difficulty was so convincing that Signor Tittoni admitted that 'the League . . . had not the right to compel a State which was not a Member to co-operate in the blockade'. His report was amended in accordance with that admission, and thus unanimously adopted.

Ever since that memorable discussion, which was resumed in the Assemblies of 1920 and 1921, continued through the debates relating to a treaty of mutual guarantee in 1922 and 1923, and which finally led to the death of the Protocol of 1924, the lack of universality of the League has paralysed all efforts effectively to organise the mutual protection of its members. This lack of universality, and notably the abstention of the United States, has naturally exercised a particularly sobering influence on the policy of Great Britain. The United States, it must be remembered, has never abandoned its traditional attitude as the champions of neutral rights in case of war. Great Britain, on the other hand, is the leading maritime member of the League of Nations. It would, therefore, be the first to suffer from the effects of an international blockade, unless assisted by all the other world powers, or at least not opposed by the mightiest of them all.

The second reason which has prevented the League from assuming fully its natural role as the guardian of peace is that, quite irrespective of the dangers of external complications, several of its members regard the present state of Europe as untenable and the present

policies of those of their fellow members who most
insistently demand guarantees as fundamentally un-
justifiable. They might even be prepared to run the
risk of external complications and to pledge themselves
unreservedly to a policy of intervention in the interests
of peace, if these interests were, in their opinion,
synonymous with those of justice. We again turn to
Mr. Garvin for a brief and convincing statement of
this difficulty. In his already quoted address he
declared:

As matters stand in Europe, or must come to stand unless
Europe does something for itself, the alleged 'aggressors'
might not be the principal offenders against wisdom and
justice. To maintain regional ascendancies by superior force
of arms in peace time—is this non-aggression? To resist
such ascendancies—is this aggression? Neither side in such
a case is likely to agree that right is on the side of the other.
Here we must think of Hegel's warning words: 'Tragedy is
not the conflict of right and wrong, but of right and right.'
Or at least of equal and opposite convictions at the time
concerning right and right.[1]

It is fortunate that, up to the present, no occasion
has arisen which clearly called for the application
of Article 16. Theoretically, therefore, it is still an
open question whether the scheme of sanctions therein
provided for would or would not work in practice.
There is no doubt, however, that the dominant opinion
in governmental and parliamentary circles, as well as
among the general staffs, is in the negative. The increasing force of national armaments is susceptible of
no other satisfactory explanation.

The outlook is undoubtedly serious, as the most convinced and far-sighted friends of the League are the

[1] J. L. Garvin, op. cit., pp. 274, 275.

first to concede. It is serious because of the radical discontent with the situation, based on international treaties as they are to-day, which prevails in many quarters. And it is serious because, in the absence of some international authority endowed with the power to alter these treaties and thereby to allay this discontent, the alternative with which we are faced is: voluntary concessions by the beneficiaries of the present situation, or war. As those beneficiaries are reluctant to exchange the limited but certain privileges, territorial and financial, which they enjoy to-day, for an enhanced but still uncertain measure of international security, the prospect of war cannot be dismissed.

The fundamental fact is that peace cannot be guaranteed to and against sovereign states by an unsovereign League. Only if the League were endowed with that kind of sovereignty to which all states, and particularly the great powers, still pretend to-day, could it enforce peace. Then, but then only, could it enforce peace, because it could enforce justice and, with the consent and support of the overwhelming majority of its members, repress all attempts to disturb peace or to maintain injustice by violence.

Peace under a strong League, or continued competitive armaments and rival alliances based on the fear of war under the present League—such is the choice before mankind to-day.

CONCLUSIONS

THROUGHOUT these pages we have witnessed the constant struggle between the principle of international solidarity, as represented by the League of Nations on the one hand, and the dogma of national sovereignty, as represented by the states of the world on the other. Whether we consider the philosophical basis of the League, the evolution of its structure, or the history of its various activities in the field of the organization of peace and the prevention of war, we are constantly confronted with the same antithesis.

In the final scene of the *Taming of the Shrew*, the heroine Katharina says:

> I am asham'd that women are so simple
> To offer war where they should kneel for peace,
> Or seek for rule, supremacy, and sway,
> When they are bound to serve, love, and obey.

Shakespeare might well have replaced 'women' by 'nations' in the first line of this passage. Only when nations will have lost the simplicity which leads them to 'offer war where they should kneel for peace, or seek for rule, supremacy, and sway, when they are bound to serve, love, and obey'—to serve, love, and obey the whole human race, and not only their own national selves—will mankind enjoy the blessings of justice and peace for all. One might have hoped that the violence and brutality of the World War would have been sufficient effectively to tame the shrews of national sovereignty. The lesson has obviously not yet been learnt. Let us hope that an increasing realization of its true significance may spare the world a repetition of its horrors.

Can we now, in conclusion, answer the fundamental question which we asked ourselves at the beginning of this inquiry: 'What is the League?'

Unless we have entirely failed in our purpose, the reader will be convinced that no simple answer can possibly be satisfactory. In all the voluminous literature on the subject we have found no brief statement more enlightening than the following, taken from Professor Elliott's *Pragmatic Revolt in Politics*, in the preface of which he declares that 'the theories of Mr. H. J. Laski, with which I have largely disagreed, have been my greatest stimulant':

It would be . . . wilful blindness not to recognize that for the present one can only hope for a voluntary recognition of the folly of this pluralistic international society with no effective limits in national duels. Coercion of great powers is not possible, till general consent makes the League an instrument of law. And general consent waits upon the abating of the exclusiveness of nations as cultural communities. In the meantime, if the League affords only a settled means of conference, that is still a great step toward limiting anarchy. . . . As a state the League of Nations and the World Court represent exactly that 'discredited State' which syndicalistic pluralism desires within the nation. The League is able to justify itself as the super-state which Mr. Laski oddly believes it to be only if the constitutional state is treated, as he treats it, as internally lacking coercive finality. . . . Actually it constitutes about the same authority in the modern feudalism of international society that the king's authority did in the area comprising France of, say, the Thirteenth Century, with perhaps some addition of the moral suasion of the Pope. The League has, theoretically, large powers of sanction, economic, military, and moral. But it has not the force at its own disposal to check this modern feudalism, any more than had the King of France of that period to hold his own greater vassals in order. . . . It is as a settled method of conference on international problems that the League has real value. Aside from that the League can proceed only to co-operative welfare work, because it is limited to matters commanding unanimity. That is not ideal; that is not, one hopes, a permanent condition. There are signs, indeed, that the sanction of the moral disapproval of such international community as already exists is becoming a real restraint on the more blatant types of international bad morals and worse manners. But the absence of final legal control is a present fact.[1]

The present League is not a super-state; so much is quite clear. Nor is it a true confederation of states, except possibly a very loose one. It is, in theory at least, if not in practice, an alliance against the outside world. And in fact it is undoubtedly a continuous international conference and a very effective public forum. Mr. Hugh Dalton has put it in a nutshell when, in his book *Towards the Peace of Nations*, from which we quoted at the beginning of these pages, he declared:

Between the pre-war international anarchy and a World State, the League of Nations is a compromise and, perhaps, a transition. An inevitable transition, if the World State is destined to be born; a pale substitute, if it is for ever unattainable. But this League, full of promise and full of imperfections, is a fact, which the World State, as yet, is not.[2]

The same fundamentally true idea has been expressed with remarkable clarity by the great British Foreign Secretary, to whom perhaps more than to any other contemporary statesman Europe and the world to-day are looking for leadership. At a dinner of the Foreign

[1] W. Y. Elliott, *The Pragmatic Revolt in Politics—Syndicalism, Fascism, and the Constitutional State* (New York, 1928), pp. 358, 482, 483.

[2] Hugh Dalton, op. cit., p. 87.

Press Association on April 24, 1931, Mr. Arthur
Henderson is reported to have said:

At present we are in the transition stage between the old
individualistic diplomacy, under which each nation or group
of nations played for its own hand, and the post-war diplomacy of conciliation and co-operation. In the old days men
and nations thought largely in terms of potential warfare,
but under the new dispensation towards which we were
striving they would, he hoped, think in terms of permanent
peace.

To think in terms of permanent peace and absolutely
to disregard the possibility of potential warfare is not
yet possible. It will become possible in the course of
time only as the nations, to-day still sovereign, gradually
learn to broaden their narrowly jealous and provoca-
tive ideal of national selfishness into the only true ideal
of human fellowship. The present League is the school
in which experience daily teaches them that, in a world
struggling towards unity, national sovereignty inevitably leads to international war and thereby to universal
suicide. Only when this lesson will have been generally
and thoroughly understood will the League of Nations,
as yet a useful but humble clearing-house of international relations, become what the impatient reformer seeks for in vain in Geneva to-day: a temple of
lasting peace built on the foundations of secure justice.

PRINTED IN GREAT BRITAIN AT THE UNIVERSITY PRESS, OXFORD
BY JOHN JOHNSON, PRINTER TO THE UNIVERSITY